TASTY *Holiday* GIFTS

*A*ll of us enjoy receiving homemade gifts from the kitchen, knowing well the love and thoughtfulness behind each one. We also take great pleasure in making holiday gifts for the special people in our lives. Creative presentations such as attractive wrappings, decorative baskets, and clever accessories complement the spirit of our offerings, sending the simple, heartfelt message: "This gift was lovingly created just for you."

Tasty Holiday Gifts *is an indispensable guidebook for those of us who want to spread the joy of giving all through the year. From New Year's Day to Christmas, you'll discover dozens of special occasions to commemorate with delicious gifts and imaginative crafts. Your favorite holidays are here, plus lots of fun, little-known observances to enrich your life. May your year be filled with many happy celebrations!*

Anne Childs

LEISURE ARTS, INC.
Little Rock, Arkansas

TASTY *holiday* GIFTS

EDITORIAL STAFF

Editor-in-Chief: Anne Van Wagner Childs
Executive Director: Sandra Graham Case
Creative Art Director: Gloria Bearden
Executive Editor: Susan Frantz Wiles

PRODUCTION
TECHNICAL
Managing Editor: Sherry Taylor O'Connor
Senior Technical Writer: Chanda English Adams
Technical Writers: Kathy Rose Bradley, Ann Brawner Turner, and Candice Treat Murphy

DESIGN
Design Director: Patricia Wallenfang Sowers
Designers: Diana Heien Suttle, Mary Lillian Hill, and Rebecca Sunwall Werle

FOODS
Foods Editor: Susan Warren Reeves, R.D.
Assistant Foods Editor: Jane Kenner Prather
Test Kitchen Assistant: Nora Faye Spencer Clift

EDITORIAL
Associate Editor: Dorothy Latimer Johnson
Senior Editorial Writer: Linda L. Trimble
Editorial Writers: Laurie R. Burleson, Robyn Sheffield-Edwards, and Leslie Mahan O'Malley
Advertising and Direct Mail Copywriters: Steven M. Cooper and Marla Shivers

ART
Production Art Director: Melinda Stout
Magazine/Book Art Director: Diane M. Ghegan
Senior Production Artist: Michael Spigner
Production Artists: Leslie Loring Krebs and Ashley Cole
Photography Stylists: Sondra Harrison Daniel and Charlisa Erwin Parker
Typesetters: Cindy Lumpkin and Stephanie Cordero
Advertising and Direct Mail Artist: Linda Lovette

BUSINESS STAFF

Publisher: Steve Patterson
Controller: Tom Siebenmorgen
Retail Sales Director: Richard Tignor
Retail Marketing Director: Pam Stebbins
Retail Customer Services Director: Margaret Sweetin
Marketing Manager: Russ Barnett

Executive Director of Marketing and Circulation: Guy A. Crossley
Fulfillment Manager: Byron L. Taylor
Print Production: Nancy Reddick Lister and Laura Lockhart

MEMORIES IN THE MAKING SERIES

Copyright© 1993 by Leisure Arts, 5701 Ranch Drive, Little Rock, Arkansas 72212. All rights reserved. No part of this book may be reproduced in any form or by any means without the prior written permission of the publisher, except for brief quotations in reviews appearing in magazines or newspapers. We have made every effort to ensure that these recipes and instructions are accurate and complete. We cannot, however, be responsible for human error, typographical mistakes, or variations in individual work. Printed in the United States of America. First Printing.

International Standard Book Number 0-942237-21-8

Table of Contents

GOOD LUCK PIE

*I*t's said that each black-eyed pea eaten on New Year's Day ensures a day of good luck in the coming year. A unique way to serve the traditional peas, this delicious Black-Eyed Pea Pie may bring just the extra luck a friend needs to help keep those New Year's resolutions! The custard-like pie is flavored with cinnamon and other spices and topped with chopped pecans. What a great new tradition!

BLACK-EYED PEA PIE

CRUST

  1½ cups all-purpose flour
  ½ teaspoon salt
  ½ cup vegetable shortening
  ¼ cup cold water

FILLING

  1 can (15 ounces) black-eyed peas,
      drained and puréed
  ¾ cup butter or margarine, softened
  3 eggs
  1 cup granulated sugar
  1 can (5 ounces) evaporated milk
  ½ cup whole milk
  1 tablespoon all-purpose flour
  1 teaspoon vanilla extract
  ½ teaspoon ground allspice
  ½ teaspoon ground cinnamon
  ½ teaspoon pumpkin pie spice
  1 cup chopped pecans

For crust, stir together flour and salt in a medium bowl. Using a pastry blender or 2 knives, cut in shortening until mixture resembles coarse meal. Sprinkle with water; mix until a soft dough forms. On a lightly floured surface, use a floured rolling pin to roll out dough to ⅛-inch thickness. Transfer to a 9-inch deep-dish pie plate and use a sharp knife to trim edge of dough. Cover and set aside.

Preheat oven to 350 degrees. For filling, beat peas and butter in a medium bowl. Stir in next 9 ingredients. Pour filling into crust. Sprinkle pecans over filling. Bake 55 minutes to 1 hour or until a knife inserted off-center comes out clean. Cool completely on a wire rack. Cover and store in refrigerator.

Yield: about 8 servings

NEW YEAR'S PARTY TIME

*R*ing in the New Year with this festive cocktail! The drink is a combination of cranberry juice, peach schnapps, and vodka. For a fun, functional hostess gift, deliver the fruity beverage in an ice bucket decorated with dimensional paint and glittery faux jewels.

NEW YEAR'S COCKTAIL

   3 cups cranberry juice cocktail
   1 cup peach schnapps
   1 cup vodka

In a 1½-quart container, combine all ingredients; stir until well blended. Cover and refrigerate until ready to serve. Give with serving instruction.

Yield: about six 6-ounce servings

To serve: Pour over crushed ice.

"PARTY" ICE BUCKET

You will need a 3-quart clear acrylic ice bucket with removable liner, paint marker with fine point, dimensional paint in squeeze bottles, jewel stones, household cement, shredded cellophane, tracing paper, and removable tape.

1. Trace pattern, page 114, onto tracing paper. Remove liner from bucket and tape pattern to inside of bucket. Outline letters with paint marker on outside of bucket; allow to dry. Paint designs on letters with dimensional paint; allow to dry. Remove pattern from inside of bucket.

2. Glue jewel stones to bucket; allow to dry.

3. Line bucket with cellophane; replace liner.

HUGS AND SQUEEZES

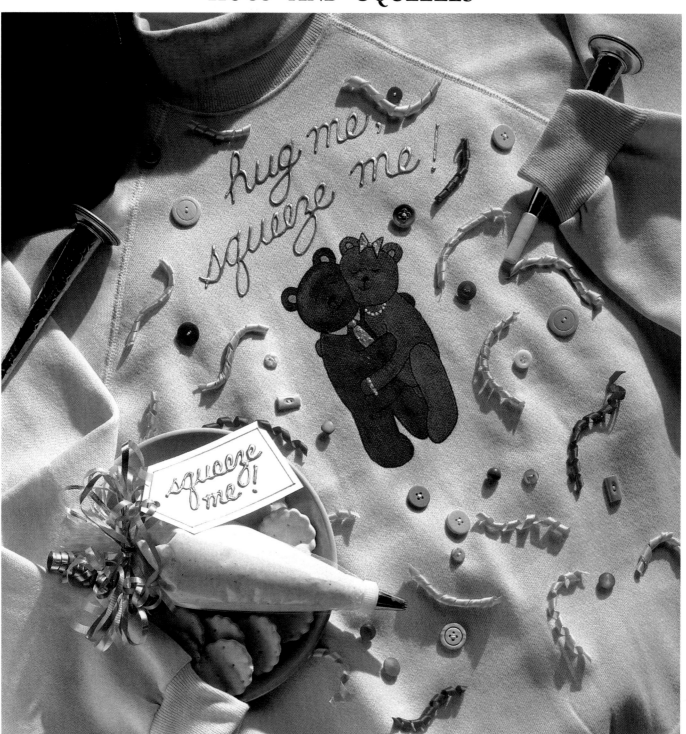

*O*n *National Hugging Day*™ *(January 21), spread warm feelings to someone special with our Squeeze Cheese Spread. This savory blend of Cheddar, Muenster, and Swiss cheeses — given in a squeezable pastry bag — makes a quick and easy snack when served with crackers. To add to the fun, present the spread with this lovable sweatshirt as a reminder that everyone can use a hug now and then.*

SQUEEZE CHEESE SPREAD

- 2 cups (about 8 ounces) shredded sharp Cheddar cheese
- 2 cups (about 8 ounces) shredded Muenster cheese
- 2 cups (about 8 ounces) shredded Swiss cheese
- 1 cup sour cream
- ½ cup white cooking wine
- 1 teaspoon Worcestershire sauce
- 1 teaspoon hot pepper sauce
- ¼ teaspoon salt
- ¼ teaspoon ground black pepper
- ¼ teaspoon garlic powder

In a blender or food processor, process all ingredients until smooth. Spoon cheese mixture into 2 disposable pastry bags fitted with large star tips. Close ends of pastry bags with rubber bands. Place in resealable plastic bags and store in refrigerator until ready to present. Give with serving instructions.

Yield: about 4 cups cheese spread

To serve: Let stand at room temperature 20 to 30 minutes or until soft enough to squeeze through tip. Serve with crackers or bread.

For tag, use dimensional paint to paint ''squeeze me!'' on white paper; allow to dry. Cut paper into tag shape. Use felt-tip marker to draw around tag ¼″ from edges. Use hole punch to punch a hole in pointed end of tag. Tie lengths of curling ribbon into a bow around top of pastry bag; thread tag onto 1 ribbon length. Curl ribbon ends.

''HUG ME'' SWEATSHIRT

You will need a light-colored sweatshirt; brown, lt brown, yellow, and lt rose fabric paint; purple and pearl dimensional fabric paint in squeeze bottles; assorted buttons; ¼″w to ⅜″w satin ribbons; thread to match sweatshirt; paintbrushes; size 7 metal knitting needles; washable fabric glue; black permanent felt-tip pen with fine point; hot-iron transfer pencil; tracing paper; removable fabric marking pen; wooden spring-type clothespins; and T-shirt form or cardboard covered with waxed paper.

1. Wash, dry, and press sweatshirt according to paint manufacturers' recommendations.
2. Trace pattern, page 114, onto tracing paper. Following manufacturer's instructions, use transfer pencil to transfer pattern to sweatshirt. Insert T-shirt form into sweatshirt. Use fabric marking pen to write ''hug me, squeeze me!'' on sweatshirt.
3. Paint bears the following colors:
   boy bear - brown
   girl bear - lt brown
   collar - yellow
   insides of ears - lt rose.
Allow to dry. If necessary, heat-set design according to paint manufacturer's recommendations.
4. Use black pen to draw over transferred lines and to color in noses. Use purple paint and paintbrush to paint tie and hair bow. Use pearl paint to paint jewelry. Use purple paint to paint over words.
5. Allow sweatshirt to dry flat for 24 hours.
6. For ribbon curls, cut ribbons into 12″ and 14″ lengths. Wet ribbon. Overlapping long edges, tightly wrap 1 ribbon length around knitting needle. Secure ribbon to needle with clothespins. Repeat to wrap remaining ribbon lengths around needles. Wet ribbons again. Place needles on a baking sheet and dry in a preheated 250 degree oven for approx. 20 minutes or until dry.
7. Glue ribbon curls to sweatshirt; allow to dry.
8. Sew buttons to sweatshirt.
9. To launder, follow paint and glue manufacturers' recommendations.

PRETTY HAT CAKE

LEMON SPONGE CAKE

Sugared flowers must be prepared 1 day in advance.

SUGARED FLOWERS
- 3 egg whites
- Edible pesticide-free flowers and leaves (we used pansies, mums, carnations, and violets)
- 1 cup granulated sugar

CAKE
- 8 eggs, divided
- 1 cup granulated sugar, divided
- ¼ cup lemon juice
- 1 teaspoon dried grated lemon peel
- 1 teaspoon vanilla extract
- ½ teaspoon lemon extract
- 1 cup plus 2 tablespoons sifted cake flour
- 1 teaspoon cream of tartar
- ¼ teaspoon salt

FROSTING
- 6 cups sifted confectioners sugar
- 1½ cups butter or margarine, softened
- 3 tablespoons milk
- 1 tablespoon vanilla extract
- Yellow paste food coloring
- Ribbon to decorate

For sugared flowers, place egg whites in a small bowl. Dip flowers in egg whites. Hold dipped flowers over a sheet of waxed paper and sprinkle generously with sugar. Place on waxed paper and allow to dry at room temperature 24 hours or until hardened.

For cake, preheat oven to 325 degrees. In a large bowl, combine 1 whole egg and 7 egg yolks, reserving egg whites. Beat 3 minutes using high speed of an electric mixer. Continue beating 5 to 6 minutes longer while adding ⅔ cup sugar, 1 tablespoon at a time. Add lemon juice, lemon peel, and extracts; beat 1 minute longer. Add flour and mix just until moistened using low speed of mixer.

Wash and dry beaters. In a large bowl, beat egg whites until frothy. Add cream of tartar and salt. Continue to beat until soft peaks form. Gradually add remaining ⅓ cup sugar, beating until stiff peaks form. Fold half of egg white mixture into batter. Fold in remaining egg white mixture. Gently spoon about 4 cups batter into an ungreased 12-inch diameter x ½-inch-deep pizza pan. Spoon remaining batter into an ungreased 1-quart (about 7-inch diameter) oven-proof glass bowl. Place pizza pan and bowl on separate baking sheets. Swirl batter with a knife to release any air pockets. Bake cake in pizza pan 25 to 30 minutes or until golden brown on top and springs back when lightly pressed. Bake cake in bowl 30 to 35 minutes, using same test for doneness. Invert cake containers onto wire racks and allow cakes to cool in containers. Remove cakes from containers.

For frosting, beat sugar, butter, milk, and vanilla in a large bowl until smooth. Tint frosting light yellow. Transfer large cake to a serving plate. Place small cake in center of large cake. Spread frosting over sides and top of cake.

To decorate cake, arrange ribbon and sugared flowers around base of crown. Remove ribbon and flowers before serving.

Yield: 12 to 16 servings

---

*T*his pretty hat is really a Lemon Sponge Cake! The delicious dessert is topped with light, creamy frosting and crowned with a ring of sugar-glazed flowers. Created in honor of Hat Day (celebrated each year on the third Friday in January), the cake is baked in two layers — one in a pizza pan, the other in a bowl — and stacked to look like a wide-brimmed hat.

"THIRST AID" KIT

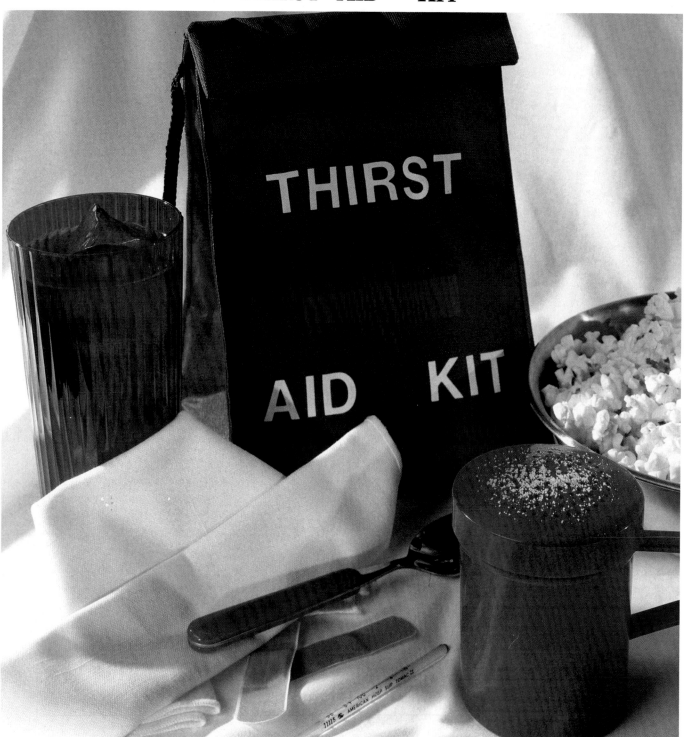

*O*n National School Nurse Day (the fourth Wednesday in January), come to the rescue of your favorite nurse with this ''Thirst Aid'' Kit! Our snack sack contains refreshing Strawberry Tea Mix, flavorful Cheese-Butter Popcorn Seasoning, and a cute ''nurse's cap'' napkin. On a busy day, this gift will be a real lifesaver!

STRAWBERRY TEA MIX

  3 cups unsweetened powdered instant tea
  1 package (0.14 ounces) unsweetened strawberry-flavored soft drink mix

In a small bowl, combine tea and soft drink mix. Store in an airtight container. Give with serving instructions.

Yield: about 3 cups tea mix

To serve: Stir 1 tablespoon tea mix into 8 ounces hot or cold water. Sweeten to taste.

CHEESE-BUTTER POPCORN SEASONING

  ½ cup grated Parmesan cheese
  2 teaspoons butter-flavored salt

In a small bowl, combine cheese and salt. Store in an airtight container. Give with serving instructions.

Yield: about ½ cup popcorn seasoning

To serve: Sprinkle desired amount of popcorn seasoning over popped popcorn.

''THIRST AID'' KIT

You will need a purchased nylon lunch sack, ¾"h vinyl stick-on letters (available at craft or art supply stores), white dinner napkin, 5" square of red nylon fabric, paper-backed fusible web, and tracing paper.

1. Trace pattern onto tracing paper; cut out. Follow manufacturer's instructions to fuse web to red fabric. Use pattern to cut cross from fabric. Fuse cross to center front of lunch sack.
2. Use vinyl letters to spell ''THIRST AID KIT'' on sack. Heat-set letters using a pressing cloth and a low iron setting.
3. For nurse's cap, fold napkin in half from left to right and again from bottom to top. For flap, fold top third of napkin down (Fig. 1). Fold top corners to center, overlapping corners slightly; pin in place, catching flap with pin (Fig. 2). Turn napkin over and fold bottom edge up 2".

Fig. 1

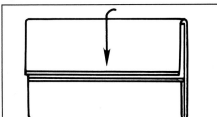

Fig. 2

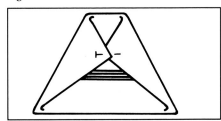

GAME-TIME SNACK

*S*urprise a football fan on Super Bowl Sunday with these Gourmet Honey-Roasted Nuts. The sweet and crunchy snacks are great for munching during the game. And when you include a pair of sporty beverage holders, your gift is sure to score extra points!

GOURMET HONEY-ROASTED NUTS

¾ cup honey
¼ cup granulated sugar
3 tablespoons butter or margarine
¼ teaspoon dried grated orange peel
1 teaspoon vanilla extract
1 cup whole unsalted macadamia nuts
1 cup whole unsalted hazelnuts
1 cup whole unsalted cashews
1 cup unsalted pecan halves
Granulated sugar

Preheat oven to 350 degrees. In a large saucepan, combine honey, ¼ cup sugar, butter, orange peel, and vanilla. Stirring constantly, cook over medium heat until sugar dissolves. Stir in nuts. Spread nut mixture on a greased baking sheet. Stirring once, bake 25 to 30 minutes or until golden brown. Cool completely on pan. Break into pieces. Roll in sugar. Store in an airtight container.

Yield: about 6 cups nuts

BEVERAGE HOLDERS

For each holder, you will need a 4″ x 9½″ piece of green art foam (available at craft stores), 7½″ of ⅛″w elastic, brown acrylic paint, white paint pen with fine point, black permanent felt-tip pen with fine point, hole punch, paintbrush, tracing paper, hot glue gun, and glue sticks.

1. (*Note:* Allow to dry after each paint step.) For football field, place foam piece with long edges at top and bottom. Use paint pen and a ruler to paint boundary lines ½″ from top and bottom edges. Paint yard lines ¾″ apart across foam. Paint 1 hash mark between each yard line. Paint yard line numbers along top and bottom edges.

2. For football, trace pattern onto tracing paper; cut out. Center pattern on foam; draw around pattern with black pen. Paint football brown. Use paint pen to paint lacing and stripe at each end of ball. Use black pen to outline stripes.

3. For each short edge, begin at top boundary line and punch a row of holes approx. ¾″ apart ¼″ from edge. Punch a second row of holes ½″ away from first row.

4. To form holder, overlap short edges, aligning holes. Glue 1 end of elastic to top inside edge of holder. Lace elastic through holes. Glue remaining end of elastic to bottom inside edge of holder.

FLAVOR OF GOOD FORTUNE

*A*n Oriental meal to celebrate the Chinese New Year is sure to bring good fortune to a friend. To help with the menu, you'll want to give a jar of our Stir-Fry Sauce — it adds spicy flavor to any stir-fried dish. We suggest including some bamboo chopsticks and a set of rice bowls. For dessert, purchased fortune cookies are a fun way to foretell the events of the coming year.

STIR-FRY SAUCE

    1 tablespoon cornstarch
    1 tablespoon water
    1 cup soy sauce
    1 cup rice wine vinegar
    ¼ cup sesame oil
    ¼ cup peanut oil
    4 teaspoons garlic powder
    ¼ teaspoon ground ginger
    ¼ teaspoon hot pepper sauce

In a small bowl, stir cornstarch and water together until smooth. In a medium saucepan, whisk remaining ingredients. Bring to a boil. Stirring constantly, add cornstarch mixture and cook 2 to 3 minutes or until slightly thickened. Cool to room temperature. Pour into an airtight container. Refrigerate 8 hours or overnight to allow flavors to blend. Give with serving instructions.

Yield: about 2½ cups sauce

To serve: Stir about 2 tablespoons sauce into about 4 cups stir-fried meat and vegetables.

For banner on basket, cut a banner shape from poster board. Use a felt-tip pen with fine point to write "The Year of Good Fortune" on banner. Hot glue banner to basket.

15

HEARTY BREAKFAST TREAT

When it's time to find out if the groundhog will see its shadow, help a friend greet the day with a good hearty breakfast! Our Homemade Sausage, freshly ground pork seasoned with herbs and spices, is a tasty addition to the morning meal. For delivery, package the sausage in our fabric wrapper — it features a tongue-in-cheek label in honor of Groundhog Day (February 2). Whether the groundhog sees its shadow or not, this humorous gift will ensure a great day!

HOMEMADE SAUSAGE

- 1 pound ground lean pork
- ¼ pound ground pork fat
- 1 teaspoon rubbed sage
- 1 teaspoon paprika
- 1 teaspoon salt
- 1 teaspoon dried crushed red pepper flakes
- ½ teaspoon ground black pepper
- ½ teaspoon ground thyme
- ½ teaspoon hot pepper sauce

In a large bowl, combine all ingredients; stir until well blended. Shape into a 3-inch-diameter roll; wrap in plastic wrap. Store in refrigerator. Give with cooking instructions.

Yield: about 1¼ pounds sausage

To cook: Slice sausage into patties and place in a skillet. Cook over medium heat, turning once, until both sides are well browned. Transfer to paper towels to drain.

"GROUND HOG" WRAPPER

You will need one 10" x 15" piece of fabric, thread to match fabric, cotton string, one 7" square of unbleached muslin, black permanent felt-tip pen with fine point, paper-backed fusible web, tracing paper, and fabric glue.

1. Use pen to trace pattern onto tracing paper.
2. For label, center muslin piece over pattern. Pulling fabric taut, pin muslin to pattern. Use pen to trace pattern onto muslin.
3. Follow manufacturer's instructions to fuse web to wrong side of muslin piece. Cut out label.
4. Press short edges of 10" x 15" fabric piece 1" to wrong side; glue in place. Allow to dry. Matching right sides and long edges, fold fabric in half. Using a ¼" seam allowance, stitch long edges together to form a tube. Turn right side out.
5. Flatten tube with seam at center back. Fuse label to center front of tube.
6. Insert plastic-wrapped sausage into tube. Tie a length of string into a bow at each end of tube.

SWEET CHERRY MUFFINS

*O*n a chilly day
during National Cherry
Month (February), warm a
friend's tummy — and heart
— by delivering a surprise
batch of these delicious
Cherry Muffins. Sweet
maraschino cherries and
chopped almonds give the
tasty treats their distinctive
flavor. Stenciled with cherries
and a checkerboard border,
the cute bread cloth can be
used year-round.

CHERRY MUFFINS

   1 jar (10 ounces) maraschino
       cherries
 1¾ cups all-purpose flour
   ½ cup granulated sugar
 2½ teaspoons baking powder
   1 teaspoon dried grated lemon peel
   ¾ teaspoon salt
   1 egg
   ½ cup milk
   ⅓ cup vegetable oil
   1 teaspoon almond extract
   ¼ cup chopped almonds

Preheat oven to 400 degrees.
Reserving ¼ cup cherry juice, drain
and coarsely chop cherries.

In a large bowl, stir together flour,
sugar, baking powder, lemon peel, and
salt. Make a well in center of dry
ingredients. In a small bowl, whisk
reserved cherry juice, egg, milk, oil,

and almond extract. Pour egg mixture
into well in dry ingredients. Stir just
until moistened. Stir in cherries and
almonds. Spoon batter into a paper-
lined muffin pan, filling each tin
¾ full. Bake 18 to 20 minutes or until
edges are light brown. Transfer to a wire
rack to cool completely. Store in an
airtight container.

Yield: about 1 dozen muffins

STENCILED BREAD CLOTH

You will need white fabric; red, black,
and green fabric paint; white thread;
tracing paper; tagboard (manila folder);
craft knife; cutting mat or thick layer of
newspapers; removable tape; stencil
brushes; graphite transfer paper; black
and green permanent felt-tip pens with
fine points; and paper towels.

1. Wash, dry, and press fabric
according to paint manufacturer's
recommendations.
2. For bread cloth, cut a fabric piece 1″
larger on all sides than desired finished
size. Press all edges of fabric piece ½″
to wrong side; press ½″ to wrong side
again and stitch in place.
3. Follow Step 1 of Stenciling, page 122,
to make 1 stencil for checkerboard
design and 1 stencil for cherry design.
4. Follow Step 2 of Stenciling, page 122,
to stencil cherry design at each corner
of cloth and checkerboard along each
edge of cloth, repeating checkerboard
as needed.
5. If necessary, follow paint
manufacturer's instructions to heat-set
design.
6. Outline cherries and draw detail lines
and stems on cherries with black pen.
Outline leaves and draw detail lines on
leaves with green pen.

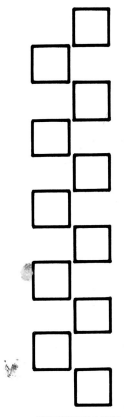

CHECKERBOARD

CHERRIES

19

FROM THE HEART

Borrowing an old European tradition, Victorian Heart Cookies capture the spirit of the true romantic. The shortbread hearts are cut out in several sizes and feature fancy paper cutouts that are held in place by the pink icing. A heart-shaped box with elegant embellishments is perfect for delivering these little tokens of affection on Valentine's Day.

VICTORIAN HEART COOKIES

COOKIES

- 2 cups all-purpose flour
- 1 cup pecans
- 1/8 teaspoon salt
- 1 cup butter or margarine, softened
- 1/2 cup firmly packed brown sugar

ICING

- 3 cups sifted confectioners sugar
- 1/4 cup milk
  - Pink paste food coloring
  - Paper cutouts to decorate

Process flour, pecans, and salt in a blender or food processor until mixture is a fine powder. In a large bowl, cream butter and sugar until fluffy. Stir dry ingredients into creamed mixture. Cover and chill 1 hour.

Preheat oven to 350 degrees. On a lightly floured surface, use a floured rolling pin to roll out dough to 1/8-inch thickness. Use various sizes of heart-shaped cookie cutters to cut out cookies. Transfer to a greased baking sheet. Bake 12 to 15 minutes or until edges are light brown. Transfer to a wire rack with waxed paper underneath to cool completely.

For icing, stir sugar and milk together in a medium bowl until smooth. Tint icing pink. Ice cookies. Before icing hardens, gently press paper cutouts on tops of cookies. Allow icing to harden. Store in an airtight container. Remove paper cutouts before eating.

Yield: about 3 1/2 dozen 2 1/2-inch cookies

VALENTINE GIFT BOX

You will need an approx. 8"w heart-shaped box, wrapping paper for side of box, fabric for box lid, 1 1/2"w satin ribbon for bow, 1/2"w satin ribbon and decorative trim for side of box lid, silk rose with leaves, desired color spray paint, white paper, spray adhesive, craft glue, and red felt-tip pen with fine point.

1. Spray paint inside of box and box lid; allow to dry.

2. To cover side of box, measure around box and add 1"; measure height of box. Cut wrapping paper the determined measurements. Use spray adhesive to apply wrapping paper to side of box.

3. To cut out fabric for lid, use a pencil to draw around lid on wrong side of fabric. Cut out fabric 1/2" outside pencil line. At 1/2" intervals, clip edges of fabric to within 1/8" of pencil line.

4. (*Note:* Use craft glue for remaining steps; allow to dry after each glue step.) To cover lid, center lid on wrong side of fabric. Alternating sides and pulling fabric taut, glue clipped edges of fabric to side of lid.

5. To cover side of lid, measure around lid and add 1/2". Cut 1/2"w ribbon and decorative trim the determined measurement. Glue ribbon to side of lid. Glue decorative trim over ribbon.

6. For bow on lid, wrap 1 1/2"w ribbon around lid and tie into a bow at top of lid; trim ends. Glue bow in place. Turn lid over; cut ribbon apart at center on inside of lid. Press ribbon ends flat against inside of lid; glue in place.

7. Tuck rose under ribbon; glue in place.

8. For tag, trace heart pattern onto white paper and cut out. Use pen to write "Happy Valentine's Day" on tag. Glue tag to bow.

TO A "HONEY" OF A FRIEND

*O*n Valentine's Day, surprise someone who's a "honey" of a friend with a sweet treat! These little heart-shaped Spice Cakes are topped with a delectable Honey Icing — and our recipe makes plenty so you can share them with lots of friends. For delivery, the cakes are placed on foil-covered cardboard hearts and wrapped with cellophane. The Cupid's arrow gift tag will send your message straight to the heart!

SPICE CAKES WITH HONEY ICING

CAKES
- ½ cup butter or margarine, softened
- 1½ cups firmly packed brown sugar
- 3 eggs
- 1 cup sour cream
- ½ cup milk
- 2 cups all-purpose flour
- 2 teaspoons ground cinnamon
- 1½ teaspoons baking soda
- 1 teaspoon baking powder
- ½ teaspoon ground cloves
- ½ teaspoon ground nutmeg
- ½ teaspoon salt

ICING
- 1 cup firmly packed brown sugar
- 1 cup butter or margarine
- ½ cup honey
- 2 cups sifted confectioners sugar

For cakes, preheat oven to 350 degrees. In a large bowl, cream butter and sugar until fluffy. Add eggs, one at a time, beating well after each addition. Add sour cream and milk; stir until well blended. In a medium bowl, sift together remaining ingredients. Add dry ingredients to creamed mixture, stirring until well blended. Spoon batter into a greased and floured pan containing 3½-inch-wide heart tins. Bake 18 to 20 minutes or until a toothpick inserted in center of cake comes out clean. Cool in pan 10 minutes. Remove cakes from pan. Cool completely on a wire rack.

For icing, combine brown sugar, butter, and honey in a small saucepan. Stirring constantly, cook over medium heat until sugar dissolves. Remove from heat; beat in confectioners sugar. Allow icing to cool 10 minutes. Gently press a 1-inch heart-shaped cookie cutter into center of 1 cake. Icing around cookie cutter, ice top and sides of cake. Remove cookie cutter. Repeat for remaining cakes. Allow icing to cool completely. Store in an airtight container.

Yield: about 1 dozen cakes

SPICE CAKE WRAPS

For each wrap, you will need medium weight cardboard; red foil wrapping paper; 20″ square of clear cellophane; red, silver, and white curling ribbon; white poster board; tracing paper; black felt-tip pen with fine point; and craft glue.

1. For foil heart, use heart pattern and follow Tracing Patterns, page 122. Use pattern to cut 1 heart from cardboard. Draw around heart on wrong side of wrapping paper. Cut out paper ¾″

outside drawn line. Clip paper at ½″ intervals to within ⅛″ of drawn line.
2. Center cardboard heart on wrong side of paper and glue clipped edges of paper to back of heart; allow to dry.
3. For tag, trace arrow pattern onto tracing paper; cut out. Use pattern to cut tag from poster board. Use pen to write the following on tag: TO A "HONEY" OF A FRIEND.
4. Center foil heart right side up on cellophane; place 1 cake on center of heart. Gather cellophane; tie ribbons together into a bow around cellophane and tag. Curl ribbon ends.

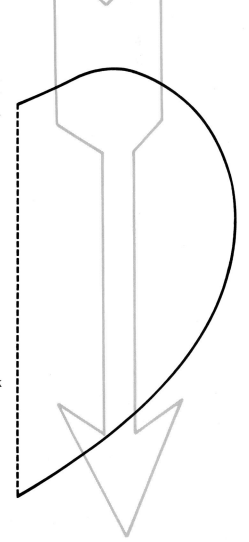

A Sweet Chocolate Valentine

Luxurious chocolates are traditional offerings for Valentine's Day, and these Raspberry Chocolates are especially nice. The marbleized candies look (and taste!) like they came from a gourmet shop — but they're easy to make in your kitchen. For an elegant gift, present the chocolates in a doily-lined basket. To coordinate with the candies, marbleize paper to create a pretty valentine.

RASPBERRY CHOCOLATES

6 ounces semisweet baking
    chocolate, chopped
6 ounces white baking chocolate,
    chopped
½ cup raspberry jelly

In separate small saucepans, melt chocolates over low heat, stirring constantly. Pour semisweet chocolate into a warm pie plate. Drizzle white chocolate over semisweet chocolate. Use the end of a wooden spoon to swirl together. Do not overmix. In batches, fill a bonbon mold half full with chocolate mixture. Using a small paintbrush, carefully brush chocolate mixture up sides of mold. Place mold in freezer 2 minutes or until chocolate hardens. Spoon about ½ teaspoon raspberry jelly into each chocolate shell. Spoon a small amount of chocolate mixture over jelly, making sure edges

are sealed. Return to freezer 2 minutes or until chocolate hardens. Invert and press on back of mold to release candies. Store in an airtight container in a cool, dry place.

Yield: about 2½ dozen 1⅛-inch bonbons

MARBLEIZED VALENTINES

For each valentine, you will need one 6″ x 10″ piece of heavy white paper, one 3″w heart-shaped paper doily, and one 13″ length each of ¼″w and ½″w satin ribbon.
You will also need 1 gallon liquid starch, one 12″ x 18″ disposable aluminum foil roasting pan, acrylic paints (we used lt pink, dk pink, burgundy, and metallic gold), plain white paper, paper towels, waxed paper, tracing paper, spray adhesive, hot glue gun, and glue sticks.

1. (*Note:* For marbleized paper, follow Steps 1 - 6.) Pour starch into pan to a depth of 1″.
2. To apply paint to starch surface, hold bottle of paint near surface and gently squeeze out a small dot of paint (paint will float and begin to spread). Repeat to apply several dots of each color of paint. Remove dots that do not spread with a fingertip or the corner of a paper towel.
3. To form marble design, use a fork or the wooden end of a paintbrush to move paint around on surface of starch, forming desired patterns.
4. Gently place a piece of plain white paper on starch surface (paper will float); immediately pick up paper by 2 corners and lay paper, painted side up, on a layer of paper towels. Using dry paper towels, blot excess starch and paint from paper. Lay paper on waxed paper; allow to dry.

5. After marbleizing each sheet of paper, remove any excess paint from starch in pan by placing a layer of paper towels on starch surface. Lift towels from starch and discard.
6. Use a warm dry iron to press marbleized paper flat.
7. Use heart pattern and follow Tracing Patterns, page 122.
8. For each valentine, match short edges and fold heavy white paper in half. Place pattern on folded paper, matching dotted lines of pattern to fold; draw around pattern. Cutting through both layers, cut out paper along solid lines only.
9. Place pattern on marbleized paper; draw around pattern and cut out. Use spray adhesive to apply marbleized paper heart to front of valentine. Use spray adhesive to apply doily to front of valentine. Tie lengths of ribbon together into a bow; trim ends. Hot glue bow to doily.

HEARTWARMING PIE

SAVORY CHICKEN PIE

CRUST
- 1½ cups all-purpose flour
- ½ teaspoon salt
- ½ cup vegetable shortening
- ¼ cup cold water

FILLING
- 2 cans (10¾ ounces each) cream of chicken soup
- 2 cups (about 8 ounces) shredded mozzarella cheese
- 1 cup frozen hash brown potatoes
- 1 pound boneless, skinless chicken breasts, cut into bite-size pieces
- 1 cup grated carrots (about 2 medium carrots)
- ½ cup milk
- 8 green onions, chopped
- 2 eggs
- 1 teaspoon dried basil leaves
- 1 teaspoon garlic powder
- ½ teaspoon ground black pepper

GLAZE
- 1 egg yolk
- 1 tablespoon water

For crust, stir together flour and salt in a medium bowl. Using a pastry blender or 2 knives, cut in shortening until mixture resembles coarse meal. Sprinkle with water; mix until a soft dough forms. On a lightly floured surface, use a floured rolling pin to roll out dough to ⅛-inch thickness. Use a sharp knife to cut a 10-inch-diameter circle. In center of crust, use a 2-inch heart-shaped cookie cutter to cut out 1 heart. Using dough scraps and a 1-inch heart-shaped cookie cutter, cut out 16 hearts. Cover all dough with plastic wrap and set aside.

Preheat oven to 375 degrees. For filling, combine all ingredients in a large bowl, stirring until well blended. Spoon filling into a greased 10-inch deep-dish pie pan. Place crust over filling. For glaze, mix egg yolk and water together. Brush egg mixture over crust. Place small hearts around edge of crust. Brush egg mixture over hearts. Bake 50 to 55 minutes or until golden brown. Cool completely on a wire rack. Store in an airtight container in refrigerator. Give with reheating instructions.

Yield: about 8 servings

To reheat: Cover and bake in a preheated 350-degree oven 40 to 45 minutes or until heated through.

GIFT TAG

You will need 1 sheet of stationery with laser-cut design at 1 corner, pink paper, spray adhesive, ⅛"w ribbon, tracing paper, and black felt-tip pen.

1. Trace heart pattern onto tracing paper; cut out. Arrange heart diagonally below design on corner of stationery. Draw around heart.
2. Trim paper ⅜" outside drawn line around bottom and sides of heart. Cut out center of heart along drawn line.
3. Use spray adhesive to apply heart to pink paper. Trim pink paper 1/16" outside heart.
4. Use pen to write "You stole my heart …" in center of tag. Make a hole in top of tag; thread tag onto ribbon.

A PATRIOTIC OFFERING

Here's a spirited gift to share with a friend on Presidents' Day (the third Monday in February)! Decorated to resemble the American flag, a loaf of flavorful Honey-Cheese Bread features stripes brushed on with red food coloring. The star-shaped butter pats are created by pressing softened butter into candy molds and chilling. Our red, white, and blue bread bag and wooden butter box also boast the stars and stripes. Even a president would be proud to receive this patriotic offering!

HONEY-CHEESE BREAD

    2 cups water
    1 cup old-fashioned rolled oats
    6 cups all-purpose flour
    ½ cup nonfat dry milk
    2½ teaspoons salt
    ½ teaspoon dry mustard
    ¼ teaspoon ground red pepper
    2 packages dry yeast
    ⅓ cup warm water
    4 ounces extra-sharp Cheddar
         cheese, diced
    ½ cup honey
    ¼ cup vegetable oil
         Vegetable cooking spray
    1 egg white
         Red liquid food coloring

In a medium saucepan, bring 2 cups water to a boil. Remove from heat; stir in oats. Cool to room temperature.

In a large bowl, stir together next 5 ingredients. In a small bowl, dissolve yeast in ⅓ cup warm water. Add oats mixture, yeast mixture, cheese, honey, and oil to dry ingredients. Stir until a soft dough forms. Turn dough onto a lightly floured surface and knead about 5 minutes or until dough becomes smooth and elastic. Place in a large bowl sprayed with cooking spray, turning once to coat top of dough. Cover and let rise in a warm place (80 to 85 degrees) 1 hour or until doubled in size. Turn dough onto a lightly floured surface and punch down. Divide dough into thirds. Shape each piece of dough into a loaf and place in a greased 5 x 9-inch loaf pan. Spray top of dough with cooking spray, cover, and let rise in a warm place 1 hour or until doubled in size.

Preheat oven to 350 degrees. In a small bowl, stir egg white and a small amount of food coloring together. Use a paintbrush and food coloring mixture to paint wavy lines on each loaf of bread. Bake 25 to 30 minutes or until bread sounds hollow when tapped. Transfer to a wire rack to cool completely. Store in an airtight container.

Yield: 3 loaves bread

BREAD BAG

You will need the following pieces torn from cotton fabric: one 6½" x 17" piece, one 16" x 17" piece, and one 8" square (for bag), and one 1½" x 27" strip (for bow); thread to match bag fabric; and tracing paper.

1. (*Note:* Use a ¼" seam allowance throughout.) Matching right sides and long edges, stitch long edges of 6½" x 17" piece and 16" x 17" piece together to form a tube. Press seams open.

2. Use pattern and follow Tracing Patterns, page 122. Use pattern to cut 1 end piece from 8" fabric square.
3. Matching right sides and raw edges, pin end piece to 1 end of tube. Stitch in place, easing to fit; clip curve. Turn bag right side out and press.
4. Place a loaf of bread wrapped in plastic wrap into bag. Tie fabric strip into a bow around top of bag; trim ends.

BUTTER BOX

You will need a 5" dia. Shaker box, 6" dia. fabric circle, 16½" each of ⅝"w and ¼"w grosgrain ribbon, craft glue, fabric marking pen, and waxed paper to line box.

1. Center lid on wrong side of fabric circle; draw around lid with fabric marking pen. Clip fabric at ½" intervals to within ⅛" of pen line. Pulling fabric taut, glue clipped edges of fabric to side of lid; allow to dry.
2. Glue ⅝"w ribbon to side of lid. Glue ¼"w ribbon to center of ⅝"w ribbon. Allow to dry.
3. Line box with waxed paper.

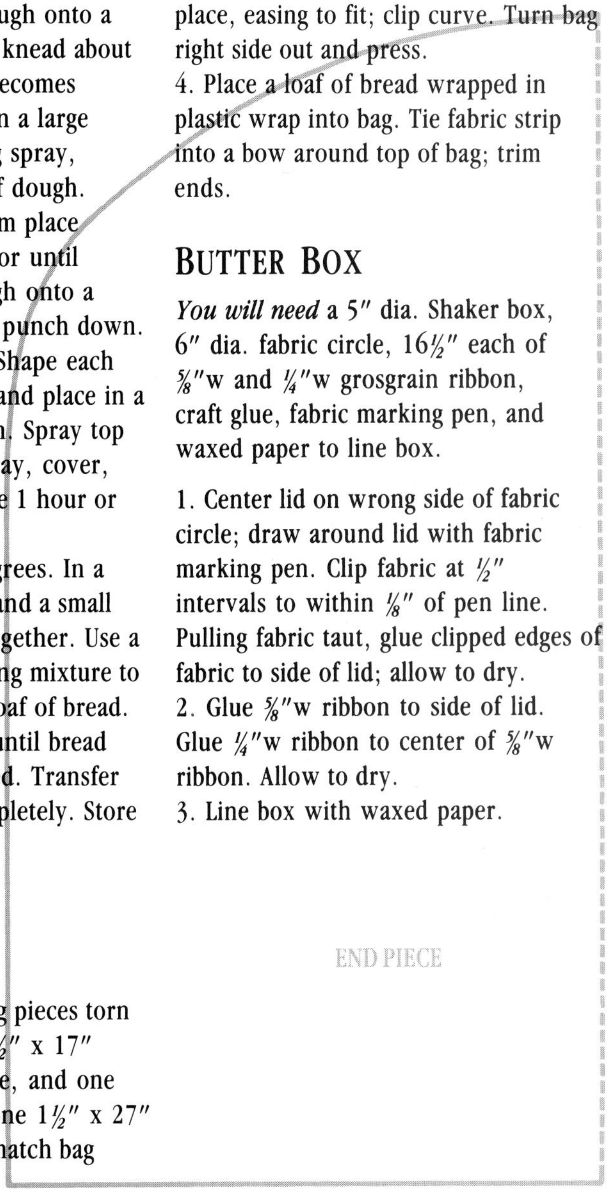

END PIECE

A DELICIOUS, NUTRITIOUS GIFT

This Barley-Vegetable Salad makes a wonderful gift for National Nutrition Month® (March). The tasty dish is a blend of crunchy vegetables, calcium-rich feta cheese, and nourishing barley. Low in cholesterol, fat, and calories, the salad is high in vitamins and minerals. For a wholesome presentation, tuck a bowl of the salad in a basket decorated with wooden carrots.

BARLEY-VEGETABLE SALAD

4 cups water
1 cup uncooked barley
¾ cup finely diced radishes
¾ cup finely diced carrots
½ cup finely diced peeled cucumber
¼ cup finely chopped fresh parsley
2 tablespoons finely chopped red onion
2 tablespoons finely chopped fresh chives
½ cup prepared oil-free Italian salad dressing
2 tablespoons lemon juice
2 teaspoons dried oregano leaves, crushed
½ teaspoon garlic powder
¼ teaspoon salt
¼ teaspoon ground black pepper
7 ounces feta cheese, crumbled

In a 3-quart saucepan, bring water to a boil; stir in barley. Reduce heat to low, cover, and simmer 50 to 55 minutes or until tender. Remove from heat; cool to room temperature.

In a large bowl, combine cooked barley and next 6 ingredients. In a small bowl, whisk salad dressing, lemon juice, oregano, garlic powder, salt, and pepper. Pour over barley mixture; stir until well blended. Stir in cheese. Cover and refrigerate until ready to present.

Yield: about 7½ cups salad

½ cup serving: 88 calories, 3.6 gms fat, 3.8 gms protein, 10.7 gms carbohydrate, 13.5 mgs cholesterol

CARROT BASKET

You will need a basket to hold dish, jumbo craft sticks for carrots, 1 regular craft stick for tag, orange acrylic paint, white spray paint, paintbrush, green raffia, white paper, green colored pencil, black permanent felt-tip pen with fine point, cutting mat or a thick layer of newspapers, craft knife, hot glue gun, and glue sticks.

1. Paint basket white; allow to dry.
2. For each carrot, use craft knife to trim 1 jumbo craft stick into carrot shape. Paint stick orange; allow to dry. Use pen to draw detail lines on carrot. Knot several 5″ lengths of raffia together at 1 end; trim short ends close to knot. Glue knot to top of carrot.
3. Glue carrots to basket.
4. For tag, cut a rectangle from white paper. Use colored pencil to write "GOOD FOR YOU!" on tag and to draw around tag ⅛″ from edges. Use craft knife to cut slits in top and bottom of tag. Insert regular craft stick through slits in tag; glue stick to inside of basket.

FRUIT SALAD DELIGHT

*O*ur tempting *"Pig Out"* Fruit Salad will be a big hit on National Pig Day (March 1). Any combination of fresh fruit is delicious served with the tangy lemon sauce — and since it's low-calorie, it's okay to *"pig out"*! For delivery, pack the fruit in our adorable *"piggy"* canister. A tag shaped like a watermelon wedge is a cute way to dress up a fabric-topped jar of the sauce.

"PIG OUT" FRUIT SALAD

   2 cups plain nonfat yogurt
   1 teaspoon sugar-free lemonade-flavored soft drink mix
   8 cups coarsely chopped fresh fruit

In a small bowl, combine yogurt and soft drink mix; stir until well blended. Store yogurt sauce and fruit in separate airtight containers in refrigerator until ready to present. Give with serving instruction.

Yield: 8 cups fruit salad

To serve: Spoon yogurt sauce over each serving of fruit.

PIG CANISTER

You will need a canister with flat lid, pink fabric, ribbon, wooden spool, lightweight cardboard, polyester bonded batting, 2 watermelon seeds, pink acrylic paint, small paintbrush, cosmetic blush, pink thread, fabric marking pencil, tracing paper, hot glue gun, and glue sticks.

1. For face, cut 1 circle each from cardboard and batting slightly smaller than canister lid. Cut 1 circle from pink fabric 1" larger than cardboard circle.
2. Center batting, then cardboard, on wrong side of fabric circle. Pulling fabric taut, glue edges of fabric to back of cardboard.
3. For ears, use pattern, page 115, and follow Tracing Patterns and Sewing Shapes, page 122, to make 2 ears from fabric. Sew final closures by hand. Gathering bottom edges of ears, glue ears to back of cardboard circle.
4. Paint spool pink; allow to dry. Glue seeds and spool to face. Apply blush to cheeks.
5. Glue face to center of canister lid. Tie ribbon into a bow around rim of canister.

READY-MADE REPAST

*O*n *International Working Women's Day (March 8), extend a helping hand to a busy woman with a good ready-made meal. Taco seasoning mix adds robust flavor to our Southwestern Soup, a hearty mixture of beef and vegetables. To help her create an authentic Southwestern atmosphere, include a set of stenciled place mats, coordinating napkins, and napkin rings trimmed with colorful dolls.*

SOUTHWESTERN SOUP

2 tablespoons vegetable oil
1⅓ pounds stew meat, cut into bite-size pieces
Salt and ground black pepper
2 teaspoons garlic powder
¼ cup all-purpose flour
1½ cups chopped onions
1 package (1¼ ounces) taco seasoning mix
2 cans (14½ ounces each) beef broth
1 can (14½ ounces) Italian-style tomatoes (do not drain)
1 package (20 ounces) frozen mixed vegetables

In a Dutch oven, heat oil over medium heat. Sprinkle meat with salt, pepper, and garlic powder; thoroughly coat with flour. Add meat and onions to oil; cook until onions are tender and meat begins to brown. Add taco seasoning, beef broth, and tomatoes; stir until well blended. Bring to a boil. Reduce heat to low, cover, and simmer 1 hour. Stir in vegetables; cook about 45 minutes or until vegetables are tender. Store in an airtight container in refrigerator. Give with serving instructions.

Yield: about 8 servings

To serve: Heat soup over medium heat until hot.

SOUTHWESTERN PLACE MATS

For each place mat, you will need a purchased rectangular fabric place mat; turquoise, yellow, red, and black fabric paint; tagboard (manila folder); craft knife; removable tape; stencil brushes; paper towels; graphite transfer paper; tracing paper; and cutting mat or a thick layer of newspapers.

1. Follow Stenciling, page 122, to stencil designs along 1 short edge of place mat.
2. If necessary, heat-set designs according to paint manufacturer's recommendations.

PRALINE PARTY BASKET

*G*et into the spirit of
*Mardi Gras with this festive
gift! The basket features
Chocolate-Pecan Pralines —
a luscious indulgence for the
day — nestled among
strands of shiny beads. A
colorful mask crowns your
gift with a bit of revelry.*

CHOCOLATE-PECAN PRALINES

2⅓ cups firmly packed brown
      sugar
  1 can (5 ounces) evaporated milk
  2 tablespoons butter or margarine,
      cut into pieces
  1 cup chopped pecans
  ½ cup semisweet chocolate chips
  ½ teaspoon vanilla extract

In a medium microwave-safe bowl,
combine sugar and milk; stir until well
blended. Drop butter into sugar
mixture. Microwave on high power
(100 %) 1 to 1½ minutes or until
butter melts. Stir until smooth. Stir in
pecans. Microwave on high power
(100 %) 6 minutes, stir, and microwave
3 to 4 minutes longer or until candy
reaches soft ball stage. Test about
½ teaspoon syrup in ice water. Syrup
should easily form a ball in ice water but
flatten when held in your hand. Add
chocolate chips and vanilla; stir until
smooth. Quickly drop by heaping
tablespoonfuls onto waxed paper. Cool
completely. Store in an airtight
container.

Yield: about 1½ dozen pralines

MARDI GRAS BASKET

You will need a basket with handle; one
4″ x 8″ piece of poster board; two
4″ x 8″ pieces of green lamé fabric;
1 yard of green string sequin trim;
approx. 4″ long purple, yellow, and
green feathers (available at craft stores);
purple, yellow, and green jewel stones;
spray adhesive; craft glue; tracing
paper; hot glue gun; glue sticks; craft
knife; cutting mat or thick layer of
newspapers; strands of beads; and gold
Mylar® gift paper.

1. Use pattern and follow Tracing
Patterns, page 122. Use pattern to cut
mask from poster board.

2. Use spray adhesive to apply mask to
wrong side of 1 fabric piece. Trim fabric
even with edge of mask. Use craft knife
to carefully cut eye openings in fabric.
Repeat to cover remaining side of mask.
3. Use craft glue to glue sequin trim
along edge and around eye openings on
front of mask; allow to dry.
4. Use craft glue to glue jewel stones to
front of mask; allow to dry.
5. Alternating colors, use craft glue to
glue feathers to back of mask along top
edge; allow to dry.
6. Hot glue mask to basket handle. Line
basket with gift paper and drape beads
over side of basket.

SHAMROCK CAKE

*T*his flavorful cake combines rich chocolate with refreshing crème de menthe liqueur. The creamy mint frosting and icing shamrocks are tinted green in honor of the day. It's a delicious way to share the luck o' the Irish!

CHOCOLATE-MINT CAKE

Shamrock decorations must be made 1 day in advance.

ROYAL ICING
- 2 egg whites
- 2⅔ cups sifted confectioners sugar
  Green paste food coloring

CAKE
- ½ cup butter or margarine, softened
- 4 ounces cream cheese, softened
- 2 cups granulated sugar
- 2 eggs
- 2 teaspoons vanilla extract
- 2 cups all-purpose flour
- ¾ cup cocoa
- 1½ teaspoons baking soda
- ½ teaspoon salt
- ¾ cup boiling water
- ¼ cup crème de menthe

FROSTING
- 4½ cups sifted confectioners sugar
- 1¼ cups butter or margarine, softened
- 3 tablespoons crème de menthe
- 1 tablespoon vanilla extract
  Green paste food coloring

To make shamrock decorations, trace patterns onto tracing paper, leaving at least 1 inch between patterns. Tape patterns onto a baking sheet. Cover with plastic wrap; secure edges with tape. For royal icing, beat egg whites and sugar in a medium bowl until well blended; tint green. Use a small knife to spread icing inside shamrock patterns. Allow icing to harden at room temperature 24 hours or until completely dry.

For cake, preheat oven to 350 degrees. In a large bowl, cream butter, cream cheese, and sugar until fluffy. Beat in eggs and vanilla. In a medium bowl, sift together flour, cocoa, baking soda, and salt. Add dry ingredients to creamed mixture; beat until smooth. Add water and crème de menthe; beat until smooth. Pour batter into 2 greased and floured 9-inch round cake pans. Bake 25 to 30 minutes or until a toothpick inserted in center of cake comes out clean. Cool in pans 10 minutes. Remove from pans and cool completely on a wire rack.

For frosting, beat sugar, butter, crème de menthe, and vanilla together in a large bowl until smooth. Tint frosting light green. Reserving ½ cup of frosting, frost between layers, sides, and top of cake.

To decorate cake, transfer reserved frosting to a pastry bag fitted with a large star tip. Pipe decorative border along top and bottom edges of cake. Invert shamrock decorations onto a flat surface and carefully peel away plastic wrap. Place shamrock decorations right side up on top of cake. Store in an airtight container in refrigerator.

Yield: 10 to 12 servings

HEARTY IRISH STEW

*S*erved in edible Bread Bowls for a satisfying one-dish meal, hearty Irish Stew is filled with chunks of lamb, potatoes, carrots, and turnips. This traditional fare is the perfect gift for St. Patrick's Day! For an extra bit of Irish charm, deliver your gift in a rustic vine basket decorated with bells of Ireland and other green trimmings.

IRISH STEW

- ¼ cup vegetable shortening
- 4 pounds boneless lamb, trimmed of fat and cut into 1-inch cubes
- 1 tablespoon salt
- 1 teaspoon ground black pepper
- ½ cup all-purpose flour
- 5 cups hot water
- 10 cups peeled and cubed potatoes (about 3½ pounds)
- 2 cups peeled and cubed white turnips (about 13 ounces)
- 2 cups chopped onions (about 2 large onions)
- 2 cups sliced carrots (about 3 medium carrots)
- 4 teaspoons dried parsley
- 2 bay leaves

In a 10-quart stockpot, melt shortening over medium-high heat. Sprinkle lamb with salt and pepper. Thoroughly coat lamb with flour. Add lamb to shortening and cook until brown. Add water and bring to a boil.

Reduce heat to medium-low, cover, and simmer 1 hour. Add remaining ingredients, cover, and simmer 30 minutes or until vegetables are tender. Remove bay leaves. Cover and refrigerate until ready to present. Give with Bread Bowls (recipe follows) and serving instructions.

Yield: about 8 servings

BREAD BOWLS

- 1 box (16 ounces) hot roll mix
- 1 cup instant mashed potato flakes
- 2 tablespoons dried minced onion
- 1⅓ cups hot water
- 2 tablespoons butter or margarine, melted
- 1 egg
  Vegetable cooking spray

In a large bowl, combine hot roll mix (including yeast), potato flakes, and onion. Add water, butter, and egg. Knead in bowl until a soft dough forms. Turn onto a lightly floured surface and knead about 5 minutes or until dough becomes smooth and elastic. Cover and let rest 5 minutes.

On a large baking sheet, invert six 10-ounce oven-proof custard cups. Heavily spray outside of cups with cooking spray. Divide dough into 6 equal balls. Shape each ball of dough over outside of a custard cup. Spray dough with cooking spray. Cover and let rise in a warm place (80 to 85 degrees) 30 minutes.

Preheat oven to 375 degrees. Bake 20 to 30 minutes or until golden brown. Cool 5 minutes. While still warm, remove bread from cups. Cool completely on a wire rack. Store in an airtight container until ready to present. Give with Irish Stew and serving instructions.

Yield: 6 bread bowls

To serve: Place stew in a large saucepan and cook over medium heat until heated through. If desired, wrap bread in aluminum foil and reheat. Spoon stew into Bread Bowls. Serve immediately.

ST. PATRICK'S DAY BASKET

You will need a basket; artificial ivy, bells of Ireland, and white hydrangea; green craft ribbon; fabric square to line basket; white paper; green construction paper; spray adhesive; black felt-tip pen with fine point; ⅟₁₆"w white satin ribbon; florist wire; hot glue gun; and glue sticks.

1. Arrange ivy around handle and front of basket; hot glue to secure. Arrange bells of Ireland and hydrangea on side of basket; hot glue to secure.
2. Form multi-loop bow from craft ribbon; wrap bow with wire at center to secure. Hot glue bow and streamers to basket. Line basket with fabric square.
3. For tag, trace shamrock pattern onto white paper; cut out. Use spray adhesive to apply tag to green paper; trim green paper ⅛" from tag. Use black pen to write "Happy St. Patrick's Day" on tag. Make a hole in top of tag. Thread ⅟₁₆"w ribbon through tag; knot ribbon close to tag. Tie tag to bow.

THE ULTIMATE CHOCOLATE CAKE

During American Chocolate Week (the third week in March), this Death by Chocolate Cake is the ultimate gift for a chocoholic! The luscious dessert features layers of rich cake and creamy filling, topped with yummy fudge frosting and lots of chocolate curls. What a delicious surprise!

DEATH BY CHOCOLATE CAKE

CAKE
- 1 box (18.25 ounces) devil's food cake mix without pudding mix
- 1 box (3.9 ounces) chocolate fudge instant pudding and pie filling mix
- 3 eggs
- 1¼ cups water
- ½ cup vegetable oil
- 1½ cups semisweet chocolate chips

FILLING
- 1 can (20 ounces) evaporated milk, divided
- 1½ cups granulated sugar
- 5 tablespoons all-purpose flour
- 4 egg yolks
- 2 tablespoons butter or margarine, melted
- 1 teaspoon vanilla extract
- ½ teaspoon almond extract
- 2 ounces semisweet baking chocolate, chopped

FROSTING
- ½ cup butter or margarine
- 6 tablespoons sour cream
- ¼ cup cocoa
- 3½ cups sifted confectioners sugar
- 1 teaspoon vanilla extract
- 1 cup chopped pecans
- 1 package (12 ounces) semisweet chocolate chips for chocolate curls

For cake, preheat oven to 350 degrees. In a large bowl, combine first 5 ingredients. Using low speed of an electric mixer, beat until moistened. Increase speed of mixer to medium and beat 2 minutes. Stir in chocolate chips. Pour batter into 2 greased and floured 9-inch round cake pans. Bake 30 to 35 minutes or until cake begins to pull away from sides of pan and springs back when lightly pressed. Cool in pans 10 minutes; invert onto a wire rack to cool completely. Slice each layer in half horizontally. Separate layers with waxed paper and wrap in plastic wrap. Freeze layers until firm.

For filling, stir together ¼ cup milk and next 6 ingredients in a small bowl; set aside. Combine chocolate and remaining milk in a medium saucepan. Stirring constantly, cook over medium heat until chocolate melts. Pour sugar mixture into chocolate mixture. Stirring constantly, bring to a boil; boil 3 to 4 minutes or until thickened. Remove from heat. Cover and refrigerate until well chilled.

Place 1 layer of cake on serving plate. Spread ⅓ of filling evenly over cake layer. Repeat with remaining filling and second and third cake layers. Place remaining cake layer on top. Cover and refrigerate until ready to frost.

For frosting, combine first 3 ingredients in a large saucepan. Stirring occasionally, bring to a boil over medium heat. Remove from heat. Add sugar and vanilla; beat until smooth. Frost sides and top of cake with warm frosting. Press pecans onto sides of cake. Allow frosting to cool completely.

For chocolate curls, melt chocolate chips in a small saucepan over low heat, stirring constantly. Pour onto a baking sheet, spreading chocolate to form an 8 x 11-inch rectangle. Refrigerate until set but not firm. To make curls, pull a chocolate curler or vegetable peeler across surface of chocolate (curls will break if chocolate is too firm). Remelt and cool chocolate as necessary to form desired number of curls. Arrange curls on top of cake. Store cake in an airtight container in refrigerator.

Yield: about 20 servings

A TIME TO RELAX

*E*veryone deserves a day just to relax, and National Goof-Off Day (March 22) is the perfect opportunity! You can treat a friend to a leisurely breakfast with our creamy Date-Nut Spread. Featuring exotic dates and crunchy pecans, the delightful spread is spiced with ginger and cinnamon. To present your gift, pack the spread in a reusable crock and tuck it in a pretty purchased bag.

DATE-NUT SPREAD

    1 package (8 ounces) cream cheese,
        softened
    ¾ cup chopped dates
    ½ cup chopped pecans
    ½ teaspoon ground cinnamon
    ⅛ teaspoon ground ginger

In a small bowl, combine all ingredients; stir until well blended. Store in an airtight container in refrigerator 8 hours or overnight to allow flavors to blend. Give with serving instructions.

Yield: about 1½ cups spread

To serve: Let stand at room temperature 20 to 30 minutes or until softened. Serve with bread or muffins.

For jar label, follow Step 3 of Bottle Bag instructions, page 56, to make label; write ''Date-nut Spread'' on label with calligraphy pen. Use craft glue to apply label to jar.

A PEPPERY SURPRISE

*Y*ou can join in the shenanigans on April Fools' Day with these tricky treats! Our Jalapeño Popcorn Balls look like the traditional snacks — but they have a peppery surprise! To distribute the hot-and-sweet morsels to friends and co-workers, place them in a basket trimmed with colorful curling ribbon and a big "April Fool!" tag.

JALAPEÑO POPCORN BALLS

    1 cup granulated sugar
    1 pickled jalapeño pepper, seeds
         removed
  ¾ cup water
  ¼ cup light corn syrup
  ½ teaspoon white vinegar
  ½ teaspoon salt
    1 teaspoon vanilla extract
  10 cups popped popcorn

In a blender or food processor, process sugar and jalapeño pepper until pepper is puréed. Butter sides of a 3-quart heavy saucepan or Dutch oven. Combine sugar mixture, water, corn syrup, vinegar, and salt in pan. Stirring constantly, cook over medium-low heat until sugar dissolves. Using a pastry brush dipped in hot water, wash down any sugar crystals on sides of pan. Attach candy thermometer to pan, making sure thermometer does not touch bottom of pan. Increase heat to medium and bring to a boil. Do not stir while syrup is boiling. Continue to cook until syrup reaches soft crack stage (approximately 270 to 290 degrees). Test about ½ teaspoon syrup in ice water. Syrup should form hard threads in ice water but soften when removed from the water. Remove from heat and stir in vanilla. Pour syrup over popcorn; stir until well coated. With greased hands, shape into balls. Cool completely on waxed paper. Wrap individually in plastic wrap.

Yield: about 2 dozen 2-inch popcorn balls

EASTER EGG SURPRISE CAKES

Beautifully decorated with tinted icing, Easter Egg Cakes have a hidden surprise inside — a yummy "yolk" made of sweetened cream cheese! A basketful of the moist cakes will enchant a friend, or you can give the cakes individually for unique little Easter treats.

EASTER EGG CAKES

CAKES
- 1 box (18.25 ounces) white cake mix without pudding mix
- 1¼ cups water
- ⅓ cup vegetable oil
- 3 egg whites (reserve 1 egg yolk for filling)

FILLING
- 4 ounces cream cheese, softened
- ¼ cup granulated sugar
- 1 egg yolk (reserved from cakes)
  Yellow paste food coloring

ICING
- 6¼ cups plus 2 tablespoons sifted confectioners sugar
- ½ cup water
- 2 tablespoons light corn syrup
- 1 teaspoon almond extract
  Pink paste food coloring

ROYAL ICING
- 4 cups sifted confectioners sugar
- 3 egg whites
  Pink, yellow, blue, and green paste food coloring

For cakes, preheat oven to 350 degrees. In a large bowl, combine cake mix, water, oil, and egg whites; beat until moistened using low speed of an electric mixer. Beat at medium speed 2 minutes.

For filling, beat cream cheese, sugar, and egg yolk in a medium bowl until smooth. Tint filling yellow. Spoon about 1 tablespoon cake batter into each tin of a greased and floured miniature egg pan containing six 3½-inch-long tins. Spoon about 1 teaspoon filling in center of batter. Continue filling each tin with batter until ¾ full. Bake 18 to 20 minutes or until cakes pull away from sides of pan and spring back when lightly pressed. Cool in pan 10 minutes. Invert onto a wire rack with waxed paper underneath to cool completely.

For icing, place sugar in a medium saucepan. In a small bowl, combine water and corn syrup. Add corn syrup mixture to sugar and stir until well blended. Attach candy thermometer to pan, making sure thermometer does not touch bottom of pan. Stirring constantly, cook over medium-low heat until icing reaches 100 degrees. Remove from heat; stir in almond extract. Tint icing light pink. Cool icing 5 minutes. Stirring icing occasionally, ice tops of cakes. Allow icing to harden.

For royal icing, beat sugar and egg whites in a medium bowl 7 to 10 minutes or until stiff. Divide icing evenly into 4 bowls. Tint icing pink, yellow, blue, and green. Transfer icings to separate pastry bags and use desired tips to decorate cakes. Allow icing to harden. Store in an airtight container.

Yield: about 2 dozen cakes

"HOPPY" EASTER

Miniature market baskets are perfect for delivering lots of "hoppy" Easter greetings! The darling bunnies are easy to make by decorating purchased sandwich cookies with almond bark, coconut, and candies. Paper ears perk up these cute creations.

BUNNY COOKIES

You will need tracing paper, white poster board, pink colored pencil, wire rack, waxed paper, disposable pastry bag, and the following ingredients:

- 1 cup sweetened shredded coconut
  Green liquid food coloring
- 24 ounces vanilla-flavored almond bark
- 1 package (1 pound) peanut-shaped peanut butter sandwich cookies
  Small, round fruit-flavored decorating candies
- ¼ cup semisweet chocolate chips

Trace ear pattern onto tracing paper; cut out. For each cookie, use pattern to cut out 2 ears from poster board. Use pink pencil to color middle of each ear.

In a small bowl, combine coconut and a few drops of food coloring; stir until coconut is tinted light green.

Stirring constantly, melt almond bark over low heat in a small saucepan. Remove from heat. Using a fork, dip cookies, one at a time, into almond bark. Transfer to a wire rack with waxed paper underneath. Before almond bark hardens, refer to photo and decorate each cookie as follows: Insert 2 ears into 1 end of cookie, gently press a small amount of coconut onto other end of cookie, press decorating candies on top of coconut for eggs, and press 1 decorating candy onto cookie for nose. Allow almond bark to harden. Place chocolate chips in pastry bag and microwave on medium power (50%) for 1 minute intervals until melted. Cut the tip of the bag and pipe chocolate onto each cookie for eyes. Allow chocolate to harden. Store in an airtight container.

Yield: about 2½ dozen cookies

EASTER BASKETS

For each basket, you will need a mini market basket, ½"w satin ribbon and rickrack for trim on basket rim, several lengths of ¹⁄₁₆"w satin ribbon for bow, fabric square to line basket, hot glue gun, glue sticks, white paper, and desired colored pencil.

1. For trim on basket rim, glue ½"w ribbon around rim of basket. Glue rickrack over satin ribbon.
2. Tie lengths of ¹⁄₁₆"w ribbon together into a bow; glue bow to basket.
3. Line basket with fabric square.
4. For tag, use colored pencil to write the following on paper: "HOPPY" EASTER! Cut paper into tag shape. Make a hole in pointed end of tag; thread tag onto 1 ribbon end.

43

EASTER EGG CASSEROLE

**T**his spicy Chilies Rellenos Casserole is a great new way to serve eggs at Easter — and it's easy to reheat for a delicious brunch dish! The quiche-like casserole features a "crust" of green chilies and a cheesy egg filling and is served with sour cream and salsa. For delivery, dress up a wicker casserole basket with colorful bunnies and eggs and include a pair of quilted Easter egg potholders.

CHILIES RELLENOS CASSEROLE

2 cans (4 ounces each) peeled mild whole green chilies, drained
1 tablespoon butter or margarine
½ cup chopped onion
8 eggs
1 cup sour cream
¾ cup all-purpose flour
½ teaspoon salt
¼ teaspoon ground black pepper
6 corn tortillas (5½-inch-diameter), cut into small pieces
2 cups (about 8 ounces) shredded Monterey Jack cheese
Sour cream and salsa to serve

Preheat oven to 350 degrees. Slit each chili lengthwise and spread open. Place in a single layer in a greased 7 x 11-inch glass baking dish. In a small skillet, melt butter over medium heat. Add onion; cook until tender. Remove from heat. In a large bowl, combine onion mixture, eggs, sour cream, flour, salt, and pepper. Stir in tortilla pieces and cheese. Pour over chilies. Bake 25 to 30 minutes or until a knife inserted in center comes out clean. Cover and refrigerate until ready to present. Give with serving instructions.

Yield: 8 to 10 servings

To serve: Cover and bake in a preheated 350-degree oven 30 to 35 minutes or until heated through. Serve hot with sour cream and salsa.

EASTER EGG POTHOLDERS

For each potholder, you will need one 10" x 24" piece of fabric for potholder, three 5" x 10" pieces of fabric for zigzag appliqués, one 1½" x 29" bias strip of fabric for binding (pieced as necessary), thread to match appliqué and binding fabrics, two 10" x 12" pieces of fusible fleece, lightweight fusible interfacing, paper-backed fusible web, tracing paper, and transparent tape.

1. Use egg top and bottom patterns and follow Tracing Patterns, page 122. Matching registration marks (⊕), overlap top and bottom patterns to form complete pattern; tape patterns together. Use pattern to cut 2 egg pieces from potholder fabric.
2. For appliqués, use zigzag pattern (shaded in yellow) and follow Tracing Patterns, page 122. Follow manufacturers' instructions to fuse interfacing, then web, to wrong side of each appliqué fabric piece. Use pattern to cut 1 zigzag appliqué from each appliqué fabric.
3. Arrange appliqué pieces on 1 egg piece, layering pieces and overlapping edges as desired. Trim pieces even with edges of egg, if necessary. Fuse in place.
4. Use a medium width zigzag stitch with a very short stitch length to stitch over raw edges of appliqués.
5. Follow manufacturer's instructions to fuse both layers of fleece to wrong side of appliquéd egg piece. Trim fleece even with edges of egg.
6. Matching edges, place egg pieces wrong sides together. Stitching close to raw edges, baste all layers together.
7. Sewing through all layers, use a straight stitch to stitch along edges of each appliqué close to zigzag stitching.
8. For binding, press 1 end of bias strip ½" to wrong side. Matching wrong sides, press strip in half lengthwise. Press long raw edges to center. Beginning with unpressed end of binding at bottom of potholder, insert raw edges of potholder between pressed edges of binding. Stitch through all layers along inner edge of binding.

EASTER BUNNY TREAT

This carrot bag full of yummy Orange Drops makes a rich reward for the Easter Bunny. The citrusy cookies, shaped like carrot "coins" and brightly iced, are a special treat that anyone would love to find on Easter morning.

ORANGE DROPS

COOKIES

- ½ cup butter, softened
- ¾ cup sifted confectioners sugar
- 1 egg
- 1 teaspoon dried grated orange peel
- 1 teaspoon orange extract
- 1¾ cups all-purpose flour

ICING

- 2½ cups sifted confectioners sugar
- 5 tablespoons milk
- Orange paste food coloring

For cookies, cream butter and sugar in a medium bowl until fluffy. Add egg, orange peel, and orange extract; beat until smooth. Gradually add flour; stir until a soft dough forms. Divide dough in half; shape each half into a 12-inch-long roll. Wrap in plastic wrap and refrigerate 1 hour.

Preheat oven to 325 degrees. Cut dough into ½-inch-thick slices. Transfer to a greased baking sheet. Bake 12 to 15 minutes or until light brown on bottoms. Transfer to a wire rack with waxed paper underneath to cool completely.

For icing, stir together sugar and milk in a small bowl until smooth. Tint icing orange. Use a fork to dip cookies in icing; return to wire rack. Allow icing to harden. Store in an airtight container.

Yield: about 4 dozen cookies

For carrot bag, place two 20″ squares of cellophane together and roll into a cone shape; use transparent tape to secure. Fill bag with cookies. Tie top of bag with green curling ribbon; curl ribbon ends. Trim top of bag.

A TRAILBLAZING GIFT

During National Reading a Road Map Week (April 4-10), help a friend hit the road with this trailblazing gift! The perfect portable snack, crunchy Pasta Trail Mix is flavored with cheese and garlic. To point your friend in the right direction, dress up the jar with a compass and send along a road atlas with a cute fabric cover. Handy pockets will keep pen, paper, and other traveling aids organized.

PASTA TRAIL MIX

- ¼ cup grated Parmesan cheese
- 2 teaspoons garlic salt
  Vegetable oil
- 1 package (16 ounces) wagon wheel-shaped pasta, cooked, drained well, and patted dry

In a small bowl, combine cheese and garlic salt; set aside. Fill a large skillet ½ full with oil. Heat oil to 375 degrees. Place pasta, ¼ cup at a time, in hot oil. Stirring occasionally, cook pasta until golden brown. Transfer to paper towels. While pasta is still warm, sprinkle with cheese mixture. Repeat with remaining pasta, reheating oil to 375 degrees between batches if necessary. Cool completely and store in an airtight container.

Yield: about 8 cups trail mix

COVERED ROAD ATLAS

You will need a 15¼" x 11" softcover road atlas, 15½" x 22½" fabric piece for cover, 8" x 8½" fabric piece for pocket, 3½" fabric square for sign, 15½" x 22½" piece of heavy white paper, 2" x 78" bias strip of fabric for binding (pieced as necessary), paper-backed fusible web, thread to match binding and pocket fabrics, two 4" lengths of ¾"w elastic, dimensional paint in squeeze bottle, and spray adhesive.

1. For cover, follow web manufacturer's instructions to fuse cover fabric piece to heavy paper. Place cover, fabric side up, with 1 long edge at bottom.

2. For pocket, press 1 short edge (top) of pocket fabric piece 1¼" to wrong side; stitch 1" from pressed edge. Press left edge ½" to wrong side. Matching raw edges, place pocket on bottom right corner of cover. Fold each elastic piece in half. Place elastic pieces 2½" apart with ends of elastic inserted ¼" under left edge of pocket piece. Sew pocket piece to cover along bottom and side edges, catching elastic in stitching at left side. For pen pocket, stitch from bottom edge to top edge of pocket 1" from left edge of pocket.

3. For binding, press 1 short edge of bias strip ¼" to wrong side. Match wrong sides and press strip in half lengthwise; press long raw edges to center.

4. To bind cover, begin with unpressed end of binding and insert edges of cover between long folded edges of binding. Stitch all layers together close to inner edge of binding.

5. For sign, follow manufacturer's instructions to fuse web to sign fabric square. Round off corners of square. Fuse sign to pocket. Paint borders and ''Road Atlas'' on sign.

6. Use spray adhesive to attach cover to atlas.

FUN FOR LITTLE READERS

*C*elebrate Reading Is Fun Week (the third week in April) by encouraging a child to read with this fun gift! Our happy pail is filled with scrumptious, easy-to-make Cinnamon-Sugar Pretzels. Since reading and snacking go hand in hand, include these colorful felt bookmarks so that little readers can mark their places while they munch!

CINNAMON-SUGAR PRETZELS

    2 loaves (one 32-ounce package)
        frozen white bread dough,
        thawed according to package
        directions
        Vegetable cooking spray
    1 cup granulated sugar
    1 teaspoon ground cinnamon

On a lightly floured surface, use a floured rolling pin to roll out each loaf to a 6 x 12-inch rectangle. Cut dough into twenty-four 1 x 6-inch strips.

Shape each strip into a 14-inch-long roll. Refer to Fig. 1 and shape each roll into a pretzel shape.

Fig. 1

Place pretzels 1 inch apart on a baking sheet sprayed with cooking spray. Spray tops of pretzels with cooking spray, cover, and let rise in a warm place (80 to 85 degrees) 1 hour or until doubled in size.

In a medium bowl, combine sugar and cinnamon; set aside.

Preheat oven to 350 degrees. Bake 18 to 20 minutes or until golden brown. Lightly spray both sides of pretzels with cooking spray. Place pretzels, one at a time, in sugar mixture and spoon sugar over until well coated. Transfer to a wire rack to cool completely. Store in an airtight container.

Yield: 2 dozen pretzels

FUN FELT BOOKMARKS

You will need desired colors of felt, two 2¾" pieces of desired color chenille stem, one ¾" piece of red chenille stem, four 10 mm wiggle eyes, 1¾" of baby rickrack, one ⅝" dia. pom-pom, seven ⅜" dia. pom-poms, compass, tracing paper, and fabric glue.

BOOKWORM

1. Trace worm pattern, page 115, onto tracing paper; cut out. Use pattern to cut 1 worm from felt.
2. Cut one 2" dia. circle from felt for head. Cut the following diameter circles from felt: 1¼", 1⅛", 1", ⅞", and ¾".

3. For eyes, wrap each 2¾" chenille stem piece around a pencil; remove from pencil. Glue 1 eye to 1 end of each stem.
4. Glue ⅝" dia. pom-pom to bottom section of worm. Glue felt circles to remaining sections of worm. Bend red chenille stem into mouth shape. Glue mouth, one ⅜" dia. pom-pom, and eyes to head. Glue head to worm.

CLOWN

1. Trace shoe, large collar, small collar, mouth, and hat patterns, page 115, onto tracing paper; cut out. Use patterns to cut 2 shoes, 1 large collar, 1 small collar, 1 mouth, and 1 hat from felt.
2. From felt, cut one 1⅝" x 7" piece for body and one 1⅝" dia. circle for head.
3. Glue hat, eyes, mouth, and one ⅜" dia. pom-pom to head. Glue rickrack and three ⅜" dia. pom-poms to hat. Glue head, collars, and shoes to body. Glue one ⅜" dia. pom-pom to each shoe.

PAINTED PAIL

You will need a white metal pail with lid, red and desired color paint pens, two large wiggle eyes, baby rickrack, tissue paper, hot glue gun, and glue sticks.

1. Glue eyes to lid. Use red paint pen to paint mouth below eyes. Use desired color paint pen to write ''READING IS FUN'' on lid; allow to dry.
2. Glue rickrack to side of lid.
3. Line pail with tissue paper.

YUMMY GLOBAL TREATS

*P*erfect for celebrating Earth Day (April 22), these cute global treats are yummy reminders to protect the environment and conserve our natural resources. The snacks are decorated to look like planet earth by coating peanut butter crackers with tinted almond bark. To share them with a friend, spruce up a twig basket with "recycled" materials.

EARTH CRACKERS

14 ounces vanilla-flavored
    almond bark, divided
Blue powdered food coloring or
    oil-based candy coloring
2 dozen purchased peanut butter
    sandwich crackers
Green powdered food coloring or
    oil-based candy coloring

Stirring constantly, melt 12 ounces almond bark in a small saucepan over low heat. Tint blue. Using a fork, dip each cracker into almond bark, coating completely. Transfer to a wire rack with waxed paper underneath; allow almond bark to harden.

Stirring constantly, melt remaining 2 ounces almond bark over low heat in another small saucepan. Tint green. Dip crumpled waxed paper into green almond bark and stamp tops of crackers to resemble continents. Allow almond bark to harden. Store in an airtight container.

Yield: 2 dozen crackers

RECYCLED BASKET

You will need a purchased twig basket, brown paper sack, newspaper, raffia, black felt-tip pen with fine point, tracing paper, graphite transfer paper, hole punch, hot glue gun, and glue sticks.

1. Cut ½"w to 1"w strips from sack. Weave strips around twigs in basket, gluing ends to secure.
2. Wrap several lengths of raffia around each corner of basket. Tie ends of raffia into a bow.
3. For tag, cut a 3" square from sack. Trace pattern onto tracing paper. Use transfer paper to transfer pattern to tag. Draw over transferred lines with pen. Write "100% Recyclable" on tag. Punch hole in top of tag. Thread tag onto several lengths of raffia and tie raffia into a bow around a twig.
4. Cut newspaper into approx. ⅛"w strips and fill basket with strips.

FOR A JOB WELL DONE

*O*n *Secretaries Day (Wednesday of the last full week in April), show your appreciation for a job well done with this ready-to-eat ham. Basted with a tangy sauce, our Mediterranean-Style Ham is delicious warm or cold — and it's a quick-and-easy entrée for a hungry family after a busy day. You'll want to include a jar of the flavorful sauce for serving, too.*

MEDITERRANEAN-STYLE HAM

- 1 cup honey
- ¾ cup rum
- ⅓ cup lime juice
- 4 cloves garlic, minced
- 1 tablespoon ground coriander seed
- 2 teaspoons salt
- 1 teaspoon ground black pepper
- 1 teaspoon ground cumin seed
- 6 to 7 pound smoked ham
- 3 cups water
- 1 tablespoon cornstarch
- 2 tablespoons water
- 2 cups chopped fresh cilantro leaves

For glaze, combine first 8 ingredients in a medium saucepan. Bring to a boil, stirring occasionally. Remove from heat.

Preheat oven to 450 degrees. Place ham in a roasting pan. Insert meat thermometer into thickest part of ham.

Pour 3 cups water into bottom of pan. Bake 30 minutes or until outside is crisp. Remove from oven. Reduce oven temperature to 325 degrees. Brush glaze over ham. Cover and bake 2 to 3 hours or until thermometer registers 185 degrees, basting ham every 15 to 20 minutes with glaze. Remove from oven; reserve meat drippings.

For sauce, stir together cornstarch and water in a small bowl until smooth. Add reserved meat drippings to remaining glaze in saucepan. Bring to a boil. Stirring constantly, add cornstarch mixture to glaze. Stirring constantly, bring to a boil and cook 10 minutes or until thickened. Remove from heat; stir in cilantro. Cover and refrigerate sauce and ham until ready to present. Give serving instructions with ham and sauce.

Yield: 12 to 16 servings

To serve: Ham may be served cold or warm. To reheat ham, place in a shallow roasting pan, insert a meat thermometer into thickest part of ham, and bake in a preheated 350-degree oven until thermometer registers 140 degrees. Stirring occasionally, reheat sauce in a saucepan until heated through. Serve warm sauce over ham.

REMEMBERING MOTHER GOOSE

*T*his Humpty Dumpty is sure to bring back happy memories. The charming fellow is really a fresh-baked loaf of bread "dressed up" in honor of Mother Goose Day (May 1). This annual celebration encourages us to pause and rediscover the enchantment of childhood nursery rhymes.

HUMPTY DUMPTY BREAD

2 cups water
⅓ cup quick cream of wheat
6 cups all-purpose flour
½ cup nonfat dry milk
2½ teaspoons salt
2 packages dry yeast
⅓ cup warm water
½ cup honey
¼ cup vegetable oil
Vegetable cooking spray

In a medium saucepan, bring 2 cups water to a boil. Remove from heat; stir in cream of wheat. Cool to room temperature.

In a large bowl, stir together next 3 ingredients. In a small bowl, dissolve yeast in ⅓ cup warm water. Add cream of wheat mixture, yeast mixture, honey, and oil to dry ingredients. Stir until a soft dough forms. Turn onto a lightly floured surface and knead 5 minutes or until dough becomes smooth and elastic. Place in a large bowl sprayed with cooking spray, turning once to coat top of dough. Cover and let rise in a warm place (80 to 85 degrees) 1 hour or until doubled in size. Turn dough onto a lightly floured surface and punch down. Divide dough in half. Shape each half into an oval and place on a greased baking sheet. Spray tops of dough with cooking spray, cover, and let rise in a warm place 1 hour or until doubled in size.

Preheat oven to 350 degrees. Bake 25 to 30 minutes or until bread sounds hollow when tapped. Transfer to a wire rack to cool completely. Store in an airtight container until ready to decorate.

Yield: 2 loaves bread

To decorate each loaf, you will need two 8½" x 14" sheets of white paper, lt tan and black paper, one 6" x 14" piece of fabric for legs, two 6½" x 8½" pieces of fabric for hat, 13" of 1½"w ribbon for bow tie, paper-backed fusible web, black and red felt-tip pens with fine points, pink colored pencil, two ⅜" dia. white buttons, two ¾" dia. black buttons, cotton string, clear self-adhesive plastic (Con-tact® paper), ⅛" hole punch, tracing paper, toothpicks cut into halves, craft glue, red liquid food coloring, small paintbrush, and purchased white decorating frosting.

1. Use head, collar, hand, and shoe patterns, page 116, and follow Tracing Patterns, page 122.
2. Apply plastic to 1 side (wrong side) of 1 sheet of white paper.
3. Use patterns to cut 1 head and 1 collar from plastic-covered paper, 2 hands from lt tan paper, and 2 shoes from black paper.
4. For face, center head over face pattern, page 116, and use black pen to trace face onto right side of paper. Use black pen to color eyes, red pen to color mouth, and pink pencil to color cheeks. Punch 1 hole at each bottom corner of head. For bow tie, tie ribbon into a bow; trim ends. Glue bow to center bottom of head.
5. For collar, use black pen to draw dashed lines along collar points on right side of paper. Glue 1 white button to each collar point. Punch 1 hole at each top corner of collar.
6. Cut two 1⅛" x 7½" pieces and one 6" x 14" piece from remaining sheet of white paper.

7. For each arm, fold 1 end of one 1⅛" x 7½" piece of paper ¾" to wrong side; fanfold remainder of arm. Glue 1 hand to 1 end of arm. Punch a hole in top of arm.
8. For legs, follow web manufacturer's instructions to fuse 6" x 14" fabric piece and 6" x 14" paper piece together. Cut two 1½" x 11¼" legs from fused material. Repeat Step 7 to fanfold legs and to glue shoes to legs. For each shoestring, tie one 7" length of string into a bow; glue bow to shoe.
9. For hat, follow web manufacturer's instructions to fuse wrong sides of hat fabric pieces together. Match short edges and fold fused piece in half. Referring to Fig. 1, fold down corners of folded edge to center and press. Fold bottom edge of hat up approx. 1" at front and back and press.

Fig. 1

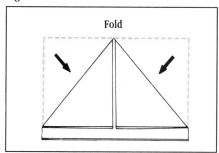

10. Referring to photo, use food coloring and paintbrush to paint stripes on half of bread. Allow to dry.
11. To assemble Humpty Dumpty, trim painted end of bread so that bread sits upright. Referring to photo, insert toothpick halves through holes to attach head, collar, and arms to bread. Use frosting to attach black buttons to bread. Place tops of legs under bread. Place hat on paper head.

DECADENT DELIGHTS

These simply sinful chocolates are as lovely to look at as they are good to eat. And the perfect time to present this elegant sampling is Eat What You Want Day (May 11). Each creamy candy is filled with coconut, caramel, chocolate, or nuts. Our pretty package helps convey the sentiment of the day — indulge yourself!

CANDY SAMPLER

9 ounces semisweet, white, or milk baking chocolate, chopped (enough for 1 recipe filling)
1 recipe desired filling (recipes follow) or ½ cup whole unsalted nuts
    Desired chocolate for garnish (optional)

In a small saucepan, melt 9 ounces desired chocolate over low heat, stirring constantly. In batches, fill desired candy mold half full with melted chocolate. Using a small paintbrush, brush chocolate up sides of mold. Place mold in freezer 2 minutes or until chocolate hardens. Spoon about ½ teaspoon of desired filling or place 1 nut into each chocolate shell. Spoon a small amount of chocolate over filling or nut, making sure edges are sealed. Return to freezer 2 minutes or until chocolate hardens. Invert and press on back of mold to release candies. If desired, decorate candies by melting a contrasting color of chocolate over low heat, stirring constantly. Spoon melted chocolate into a pastry bag fitted with a very small round tip. Pipe chocolate onto each candy. Allow chocolate to harden. Store in an airtight container in a cool, dry place.

Yield: about 2 dozen 1⅛-inch bonbons

CHOCOLATE FILLING

½ cup semisweet chocolate chips
1 tablespoon whipping cream
2 teaspoons butter or margarine

In a small saucepan, combine all ingredients. Stirring constantly, cook over low heat until smooth. Cover and cool to room temperature. Use in recipe for Candy Sampler.

Yield: enough for 2 dozen 1⅛-inch bonbons

COCONUT FILLING

½ cup sweetened flaked coconut
¼ cup granulated sugar
¼ cup light corn syrup
⅛ teaspoon salt
⅛ teaspoon coconut extract

In a small saucepan, combine coconut, sugar, corn syrup, and salt. Stirring constantly, cook over medium heat 3 to 5 minutes or until sugar dissolves and filling thickens. Remove from heat; stir in coconut extract. Cover and cool to room temperature. Use in recipe for Candy Sampler.

Yield: enough for 2 dozen 1⅛-inch bonbons

CARAMEL FILLING

2 0 caramel candies
1 tablespoon plus 1 teaspoon water
1 teaspoon vanilla extract

In a medium saucepan, combine caramels and water. Stirring occasionally, cook over medium-low heat until caramels are melted. Remove from heat; stir in vanilla. Cover and cool to room temperature. Use in recipe for Candy Sampler.

Yield: enough for 2 dozen 1⅛-inch bonbons

For box, follow Gift Box 1 instructions, page 122, to cover box with glossy white wrapping paper. We used a 1½" x 4" x 12" box and decorated it with ribbon and artificial flowers.

"RUN FOR THE ROSES" PUNCH

*H*ere's a winning hostess gift for a Kentucky Derby Day party (the first Saturday in May). Fruity and minty, our drink mix is combined with lemon-lime soda to create refreshing "Run for the Roses" Punch. In keeping with the party theme, deliver the mix in a floral bag, along with instructions for making the punch.

"RUN FOR THE ROSES" PUNCH MIX

- 1 can (46 ounces) pineapple juice
- 1 can (12 ounces) frozen limeade concentrate, thawed
- 2 cups water
- 1 cup rum
- 1 cup peppermint schnapps
  Green liquid food coloring

In a 3-quart container, combine first 5 ingredients; tint green. Pour evenly into two 1½-quart or 1.5-liter containers. Cover and store in refrigerator. Give instructions for making punch with each container.

Yield: 3 quarts drink mix, enough to make 2 recipes of punch

To make punch: In a large punch bowl, stir together 1½ quarts chilled drink mix and 12 ounces chilled lemon-lime soft drink. If desired, add ice cubes and garnish with fresh mint.

Yield: about nine 6-ounce servings

BOTTLE BAG

For a bag to fit a 1.5-liter bottle, you will need one 7½" x 42½" fabric piece, thread to match fabric, desired ribbons for bow, gold cord, 3 colors of paper for tag, calligraphy pen, ⅛" hole punch, and spray adhesive.

1. Use fabric and follow Step 2 of Fabric Bag instructions, page 122. Press top edge of bag ¼" to wrong side; press 4" to wrong side again. Stitch in place. Follow Step 4 of Fabric Bag instructions, page 122.

2. Place bottle in bag. Tie ribbon lengths together into a bow around top of bag; trim ends.

3. For layered tag, cut a rectangle from 1 color of paper. Use pen to write the following on tag: "Run for the Roses" Punch. Use spray adhesive to apply tag to second color of paper; trim paper ⅛" from tag. Repeat to apply tag to remaining color of paper.

4. Punch a hole in top left corner of tag. Thread tag onto cord; knot ends of cord. Hang tag over bow.

A CAKE THAT MEASURES UP

A gift of scrumptious Pineapple Pound Cake will tip the scales in your favor on Weights and Measures Day (May 20)! Topped with a lemony pineapple glaze, the moist cake is loaded with chunks of candied pineapple and chopped walnuts. This rich dessert really "measures up" to the occasion.

PINEAPPLE POUND CAKE

CAKE

 1 cup butter or margarine, softened
 ½ cup vegetable shortening
 3 cups granulated sugar
 5 eggs
 3 cups all-purpose flour
 ½ teaspoon baking powder
 1 cup milk
 1 cup chopped candied pineapple
   (about 8 ounces)
 ½ cup chopped walnuts
 1 teaspoon vanilla extract

GLAZE

 ½ cup pineapple jam or preserves
 2 tablespoons lemon juice

For cake, preheat oven to 325 degrees. In a large bowl, cream butter, shortening, and sugar until fluffy. Add eggs, one at a time, beating well after each addition. In a medium bowl, sift together flour and baking powder. Add dry ingredients alternately with milk to creamed mixture. Stir in pineapple, walnuts, and vanilla. Spoon batter into a greased and floured 10-inch tube pan. Bake 1 hour 35 minutes to 1 hour 40 minutes or until a toothpick inserted in center of cake comes out clean. Cool in pan 10 minutes; remove from pan and cool completely on a wire rack.

For glaze, combine jam and lemon juice in a small saucepan. Stirring constantly, cook over low heat until jam melts. Spread over top of cake. Allow glaze to cool completely. Store in an airtight container.

Yield: about 20 servings

ROSES FOR MOTHER

ROSE PETAL TEA CAKES

Sugared Rose Petals must be made 1 day in advance.

SUGARED ROSE PETALS

- 2 egg whites
  Rose petals from pesticide-free blossoms, washed and patted dry
  Granulated sugar

CAKES

- ½ cup butter or margarine, softened
- 4 ounces cream cheese, softened
- 1 cup granulated sugar
- 2 eggs
- ½ cup sour cream
- 2 tablespoons milk
- 1 tablespoon rose flower water (available at gourmet food stores)
- 1⅔ cups all-purpose flour
- ½ teaspoon baking soda
- ½ teaspoon baking powder
- ½ teaspoon ground nutmeg
- ¼ teaspoon salt
- 1 cup chopped pecans
  Pink paste food coloring (optional)

FROSTING

- 1 cup whipping cream
- 1 package (8 ounces) cream cheese, softened
- ¼ cup granulated sugar
- 1 tablespoon rose flower water
  Silk rose leaves to decorate

For sugared rose petals, place egg whites in a small bowl. Dip rose petals in egg whites. Hold dipped rose petals over a sheet of waxed paper and sprinkle generously with sugar. Transfer to waxed paper-covered rolling pin to retain shape of petals. Allow to dry at room temperature 24 hours or until hardened.

For cakes, preheat oven to 350 degrees. In a large bowl, cream butter, cream cheese, and sugar until fluffy. Add eggs, sour cream, milk, and rose flower water; stir until smooth. In a medium bowl, sift together flour, baking soda, baking powder, nutmeg, and salt. Add dry ingredients to creamed mixture, stirring until smooth. Stir in pecans. If desired, tint batter light pink. Pour into a greased and floured shortcake pan, filling each tin ⅔ full. Bake 15 to 20 minutes, using a toothpick to test for doneness. Cool in pan 10 minutes. Remove from pan and cool completely on a wire rack.

For frosting, place a medium bowl and beaters from an electric mixer in freezer until well chilled. In chilled bowl, beat cream until soft peaks form; refrigerate. In a large bowl, beat cream cheese, sugar, and rose flower water until fluffy. Gradually add whipped cream to cream cheese mixture; beat until smooth and stiff peaks form. Frost tops of cakes. To decorate, arrange rose petals and silk leaves on tops of cakes. Cover and refrigerate until ready to present. Remove leaves before eating.

Yield: about 1 dozen tea cakes

MOTHER'S DAY CORSAGE

You will need desired silk flowers (we used 1 large rose, 2 medium roses, mini rosebuds, and lilacs), 32-gauge spool wire, 1 yd of 1"w wired ribbon, corsage pin, wire cutters, and hot glue gun and glue sticks (optional).

1. Cut stems to 6". Arrange flowers as desired. Wrap stems together with wire to secure. Trim stems even. Secure flowers with glue if necessary.
2. Tie ribbon into a double-loop bow around stems; trim and arrange streamers.
3. Insert pin into back of corsage.

Reminiscent of the lavishly adorned straw bonnets that ladies once favored, these candy Marzipan Hats make a lovely remembrance for Mother's Day. The sweet treats are shaped from an almond confection and trimmed with silk flowers and ribbons of frosting. To make your presentation especially memorable, craft a keepsake miniature "hatbox" to hold each creation.

MARZIPAN HATS

MARZIPAN

- 3½ cups sifted confectioners sugar, divided
- 1⅓ cups slivered almonds, finely ground
- 3 tablespoons water
- 1 teaspoon almond extract
  Yellow paste food coloring

FROSTING

- ⅔ cup butter or margarine, softened
- 2 tablespoons milk
- 2 teaspoons vanilla extract
- 2¼ cups sifted confectioners sugar
  Blue paste food coloring
  Small silk flowers to decorate

For marzipan, combine 1⅓ cups sugar, almonds, water, and almond extract in a medium bowl; beat until well blended using an electric mixer. Beat in remaining sugar. Knead in bowl until dough sticks together. Tint marzipan light yellow by kneading in food coloring. For each hat brim, shape about 2 tablespoons marzipan into a 3-inch diameter circle. For each hat crown, shape about 1 tablespoon marzipan into a half ball. Keep remaining marzipan covered while working. Gently press each crown of hat onto center of each hat brim. Cover hats with plastic wrap and refrigerate.

For frosting, beat first 4 ingredients together in a large bowl until smooth. Tint frosting blue. Transfer frosting to a pastry bag fitted with a small ribbon tip. Pipe ribbon and bow on each hat. Arrange small silk flowers on each hat. Store in an airtight container in refrigerator until ready to present. Remove flowers before eating.

Yield: about nine 3-inch diameter marzipan hats

MINIATURE HATBOXES

For each hatbox, you will need a 3¼" dia. Shaker box, dollhouse wallpaper or wrapping paper, 11" of desired ribbon and lace trim for side of box lid, 25" of desired ribbon(s) for bow, patterned netting for box lining, mini silk rosebuds (optional), and craft glue.

Note: Allow to dry after each glue step.

1. To cover side of box, measure around box and add ½"; measure height of box and add ½". Cut a strip of wallpaper the determined measurements. With 1 long edge of wallpaper even with top edge of box, glue strip around box.
2. At ½" intervals, clip wallpaper extending beyond bottom of box to within 1/16" of box. Glue clipped edges of wallpaper to bottom of box.
3. To cut out paper for lid, use a pencil to draw around lid on wrong side of wallpaper. Cut out wallpaper ⅜" outside pencil line. Clip wallpaper at ½" intervals to within 1/16" of pencil line.
4. To cover lid, center lid on wrong side of wallpaper. Alternating sides, glue clipped edges of wallpaper to side of lid.
5. To cover side of lid, glue 11" length of ribbon to side of lid. Glue lace over ribbon.
6. Line box with netting. Place 1 marzipan hat in box. Replace lid and tie ribbon(s) into a bow around box. Tuck rosebuds under bow, if desired.

A Gift To Hit The Spot

*D*uring *June Dairy Month, help a friend create a delicious dairy dessert with our Peach-Amaretto Yogurt Flavoring. It turns plain vanilla yogurt into an extra-special treat! For a "dairy" delightful presentation, dress up a plain white gift bag with miniature cow bells and "cow spots" cut from black wrapping paper.*

PEACH-AMARETTO YOGURT FLAVORING

> 1 jar (18 ounces) peach jam or preserves
> ¼ cup amaretto liqueur
> ¼ cup chopped pecans
> ⅛ teaspoon amaretto-flavored oil (used for candy making)

In a small saucepan, melt jam over low heat, stirring occasionally. Remove from heat. Add liqueur, pecans, and amaretto-flavored oil; stir until well blended. Store in an airtight container in refrigerator. Give with serving instructions.

Yield: about 1¾ cups yogurt flavoring

To serve: Stir ¼ cup yogurt flavoring into one 8-ounce carton vanilla-flavored yogurt.

For gift bag, cut desired cow spots from glossy black wrapping paper. Use spray adhesive to apply spots to a purchased white gift bag. Tie a length of braided jute trim into a bow; tie 1 miniature cow bell to each end of jute. Hot glue bow to bag.

A Sweet Thank-You

*S*ay *"thanks" to a great group of volunteers with a batch of this sweet, creamy Coconut Fudge and our cute pins. International Volunteers Week (celebrated annually June 1-7) is a time to appreciate all those people who give freely of their time to help others.*

COCONUT FUDGE

2¼ cups granulated sugar
 1 can (8½ ounces) cream of
    coconut
 1 cup evaporated milk
 2 tablespoons light corn syrup
 1 tablespoon butter or margarine
 1 teaspoon vanilla extract
 1 cup sweetened shredded coconut

Butter sides of a large heavy saucepan or Dutch oven. Combine sugar, cream of coconut, evaporated milk, corn syrup, and butter in pan. Stirring constantly, cook over medium-low heat until sugar dissolves. Using a pastry brush dipped in hot water, wash down any sugar crystals on sides of pan. Attach candy thermometer to pan, making sure thermometer does not touch bottom of pan. Increase heat to medium and bring to a boil. Do not stir while syrup is boiling. Continue to cook until syrup reaches soft ball stage (approximately 234 to 240 degrees). Test about ½ teaspoon syrup in ice water. Syrup should easily form a ball in ice water but flatten when held in your hand. Remove from heat; add vanilla. Do not stir until syrup cools to approximately 200 degrees. Using medium speed of an electric mixer, beat fudge until thickened and no longer glossy. Stir in coconut. Pour into a buttered 7 x 11-inch pan. Cool completely. Cut into 1-inch squares. Store in an airtight container in refrigerator.

Yield: about 5 dozen pieces fudge

VOLUNTEER PINS

For each pin, you will need white poster board, gold spray paint, pin back, compass, and craft glue.

1. Spray paint both sides of poster board; allow to dry. Use compass to draw a 3″ dia. circle on poster board; cut out.

2. Make a photocopy of pattern on desired colored paper; cut out. Glue photocopied design to center of gold circle.

3. Glue pin back to back of poster board.

A Gift For Teacher

On the last day of school, this thoughtful gift will leave your child's teacher with fond memories of the year. Our easy recipe makes lots of chewy old-fashioned Oatmeal-Chocolate Chip Bars, so there'll be plenty to share with the class. To accompany the cookies, there's a cute handmade frame for displaying the class picture — a lasting reminder of a great group of students!

OATMEAL-CHOCOLATE CHIP BARS

½ cup butter or margarine, softened
½ cup firmly packed brown sugar
1 egg
½ teaspoon vanilla extract
½ teaspoon almond extract
½ cup all-purpose flour
½ teaspoon baking soda
¼ teaspoon salt
1¼ cups old-fashioned rolled oats
1 package (6 ounces) semisweet chocolate chips

Preheat oven to 350 degrees. In a medium bowl, cream butter and sugar until fluffy. Add egg and extracts, stirring until well blended. In a small bowl, stir together flour, baking soda, and salt. Add flour mixture to creamed mixture, stirring until well blended. Stir in oats and chocolate chips. Spread batter in a greased 7 x 11-inch baking pan. Bake 20 to 25 minutes or until golden brown. While still warm, cut into 1 x 2-inch bars. Cool completely in pan. Store in an airtight container.

Yield: about 3 dozen bars

SCHOOL FRAME

You will need a purchased pre-cut 8″ x 10″ framing mat with 4½″ x 6½″ opening, medium weight cardboard, 10″ x 12″ piece of fabric for frame back, 2½″ x 11″ piece of fabric for easel, items to decorate frame (we used pencils, a miniature apple magnet and a notepad, a fabric-covered wooden heart cutout with a paper tag, a painted miniature wooden book, and painted wooden letters), matte Mod Podge® sealer, high gloss clear epoxy coating (we used Aristocrat™ Epoxy Thick Crystal Clear Coating), foam brush, tracing paper, 3″ of ½″w ribbon, spring-type clothespins, and craft glue.

1. (*Note:* Use craft glue for all gluing. Allow to dry after each glue step.) Arrange decorative items on mat as desired; glue to secure.
2. Allowing to dry between coats, apply 2 coats of Mod Podge® sealer to mat front including edges.
3. (*Note:* Read all epoxy coating instructions before beginning.) Carefully following manufacturer's instructions, apply coating to mat front; allow to dry.
4. For frame back, cut an 8″ x 10″ piece from cardboard. Center cardboard on wrong side of 10″ x 12″ fabric piece. Fold fabric edges to back of cardboard; glue to secure.
5. For easel, trace pattern onto tracing paper; cut out. Use pattern to cut 1 easel from cardboard.
6. To cover easel, center easel on wrong side of 2½″ x 11″ fabric piece. Fold short edges of fabric piece over easel; glue to secure. Trimming as necessary, glue long edges of fabric to wrong side of easel. Fold easel to right side where indicated on pattern by dotted line. With bottom edges even, center wrong side of easel on covered side of frame back; glue area above dotted line to frame back.
7. For easel support, glue 1 end of ribbon to wrong side of easel where indicated by **x** on pattern. Glue remaining end of ribbon to frame back.
8. With wrong sides together and leaving 1 edge open to insert picture, glue mat and frame back together along edges; secure with clothespins. Allow to dry.

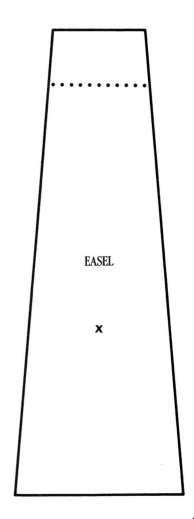

EASEL

x

YO-YO NOSTALGIA

Celebrate National Yo-Yo Day (June 6) with a friend who's still a child at heart. Our edible toy treats are sure to bring back memories of "walking the dog" with a yo-yo, shooting marbles, and playing ball. The delicious goodies are made from vanilla-flavored cookies sandwiched together with orange cream filling.

YO-YO COOKIES

COOKIES

- ½ cup butter or margarine, softened
- ⅓ cup corn syrup
- 1½ cups granulated sugar
- 1 egg
- 1 teaspoon vanilla extract
  Orange paste food coloring
- 2¾ cups all-purpose flour
- 2 teaspoons baking soda
- ¼ teaspoon salt

FILLING

- 3 cups sifted confectioners sugar
- 1 cup butter or margarine, softened
- 1 teaspoon dried grated orange peel
- 1 teaspoon orange extract
  White cotton string to decorate

For cookies, preheat oven to 375 degrees. In a large bowl, cream butter, corn syrup, and sugar until fluffy. Add egg and vanilla; beat until smooth. Tint orange. In a medium bowl, stir together flour, baking soda, and salt. Add dry ingredients to creamed mixture; stir until a soft dough forms. Divide dough in half. On a lightly floured surface, use a floured rolling pin to roll out each half of dough to ¼-inch thickness. Use a 1½-inch round cookie cutter to cut out cookies. Place cookies 1 inch apart on a greased baking sheet. Bake 5 to 7 minutes or until edges are light brown. Transfer to a wire rack to cool completely.

For filling, beat all ingredients together in a medium bowl until smooth. Spread filling generously on half of cookies; top with remaining cookies. For each yo-yo string, cut a 20″ length of string. Tie one end into a small loop. Wrap remaining end around cookie. Store in an airtight container. Remove string before eating cookie.

Yield: about 3 dozen cookies

RED, WHITE, AND BLUE DESSERT

Give three cheers for the red, white, and blue with this Patriotic Dessert! Perfect for Flag Day (June 14), the delectable treat features fresh strawberries and blueberries layered with a rich mixture of cream cheese and whipped cream. A handsome bowl makes an attractive, reusable gift for your hostess.

PATRIOTIC DESSERT

    2 cups whipping cream
    2 packages (8 ounces each) cream
         cheese, softened
    ½ cup granulated sugar
    ½ teaspoon almond extract
    2 quarts fresh strawberries, halved
    2 quarts fresh blueberries

Place a large bowl and beaters from an electric mixer in freezer until well chilled. In chilled bowl, beat cream until soft peaks form. In another large bowl, beat cream cheese, sugar, and almond extract until fluffy. Gradually add whipped cream to cream cheese mixture; beat until smooth and stiff peaks form.

For garnish, reserve about 20 strawberry halves and ½ cup blueberries. In a trifle bowl (we used a 5-inch-high x 8-inch-diameter bowl) or large glass container, layer whipped cream mixture and remaining

strawberries and blueberries, ending with whipped cream mixture. Garnish top with strawberry halves and blueberries to resemble a flag. Cover and refrigerate until ready to present.

Yield: about 16 servings

BASEBALL COOKIES

*T*he whole team will cheer for these tasty treats during National Little League Baseball Week (the week beginning with the second Monday in June)! Decorated to look like baseballs, our peanut butter cookies are guaranteed to delight your favorite aspiring major leaguers. For a sure hit, present the snacks in our cute gift sacks. They can be personalized by adding baseball pins with the little players' own numbers!

BASEBALL COOKIES

COOKIES

1 cup butter or margarine, softened
⅓ cup butter-flavored shortening
⅓ cup peanut oil
2 cups granulated sugar
2 eggs
1 teaspoon vanilla extract
1 cup smooth peanut butter
5 cups all-purpose flour
½ teaspoon salt

ICING

5 cups sifted confectioners sugar
8 tablespoons milk
Red purchased decorating icing

For cookies, preheat oven to 350 degrees. In a large bowl, cream first 4 ingredients until fluffy. Add eggs and vanilla; beat until smooth. Stir in peanut butter. In another large bowl, stir together flour and salt. Add dry ingredients to creamed mixture; stir until a soft dough forms. On a lightly floured surface, use a floured rolling pin to roll out dough to ¼-inch thickness. Use a 3-inch round cookie cutter to cut out cookies. Transfer to a greased baking sheet. Bake 10 to 12 minutes or until golden brown. Transfer to a wire rack with waxed paper underneath to cool completely.

For icing, stir together sugar and milk in a small bowl until smooth. Ice

cookies. Allow icing to harden. Use a small round tip to pipe red icing on cookies to resemble stitching on baseballs. Allow icing to harden. Store in an airtight container.

Yield: about 5 dozen cookies

For each baseball pin and sack, paint a round wooden cutout with white acrylic paint; allow to dry. Use permanent felt-tip pens to draw red stitching and to write black number on cutout. Hot glue a pin back to back of cutout. Use a white paint pen to write ''Let's Play Ball!'' and to draw baseball diamond on a purchased sack. Outline bases and draw over letters with black pen.

REFRESHING FRUIT COOLER

*H*elp a friend greet the first day of summer with a big jug of our citrusy Fruit Cooler Drink — it's a great refresher on hot, sunny days. To add to the fun, include a pair of decorated canvas shoes for strolling in style and a matching visor to shade her eyes.

FRUIT COOLER DRINK

1 can (46 ounces) pineapple juice
1 jar (40 ounces) peach juice
1 can (12 ounces) frozen orange
   juice concentrate, thawed
1 cup grapefruit juice
1 can (16 ounces) pineapple
   chunks

In a 1-gallon container, combine all ingredients. Cover and refrigerate until well chilled. Serve over ice.

Yield: about twenty 6-ounce servings

SUNNY SHOES AND VISOR

You will need a pair of white canvas slip-on shoes, yellow plastic sun visor, pink and green art foam (available at craft stores), white and yellow paint pens, six 1¾" lengths of purple plastic lacing, tracing paper, ⅛" hole punch, hot glue gun, and glue sticks.

1. Trace patterns onto tracing paper; cut out. Use patterns to cut 3 flowers from pink foam and 6 leaves from green foam. Referring to pattern, punch holes in each flower.
2. For each flower, thread 1 length of lacing diagonally through 2 holes. Glue ends of lacing to wrong side of flower.

Repeat to thread a second length of lacing through remaining holes. Glue 2 leaves to wrong side of flower.
3. For shoes, use yellow paint pen to paint dots on toe of each shoe; allow to dry. Glue 1 flower to each shoe.
4. For visor, use white paint pen to paint dots on visor; allow to dry. Glue remaining flower to visor.

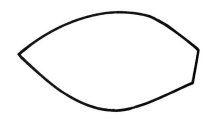

A PIE FOR DAD

For a gift that says "Dad" in a big way, bake a luscious Cherry-Amaretto Pie for Father's Day. The rich pie is made with dried cherries and laced with almond-flavored liqueur. Pastry cutouts transform the top crust into a cute shirt and tie. Dad won't be able to resist this sweet offering!

CHERRY-AMARETTO PIE

FILLING
2 cups dried cherries (available at gourmet food stores)
1 cup amaretto
1⅓ cups granulated sugar
3 tablespoons cornstarch
2 tablespoons butter or margarine, melted
¼ teaspoon almond extract

CRUST
2 cups all-purpose flour
1 teaspoon salt
¾ cup vegetable shortening
½ cup cold water

PASTRY DECORATIONS
1½ cups all-purpose flour
½ teaspoon salt
½ cup vegetable shortening
¼ cup cold water

GLAZE
1 egg
1 tablespoon milk
Red liquid food coloring

For filling, combine cherries and amaretto in a small bowl. Cover and set aside 8 hours or overnight.

Reserving 2 tablespoons amaretto, drain cherries. In a large bowl, combine cherries, reserved amaretto, sugar, cornstarch, butter, and almond extract; stir until well blended.

For crust, stir together flour and salt in a medium bowl. Using a pastry blender or 2 knives, cut in shortening until mixture resembles coarse meal. Sprinkle with water; mix until a soft dough forms. Divide dough in half. On a lightly floured surface, use a floured rolling pin to roll out one-half of dough to ⅛-inch thickness. Transfer to an ungreased 9-inch pie plate and use a sharp knife to trim edge of dough. For top crust, roll out remaining dough to ⅛-inch thickness. Use a sharp knife to cut an 11-inch diameter circle. Spoon filling into crust. Place top crust over filling. Fold edge of top crust under edge of bottom crust. Pinch edges together to seal. Cover and set aside.

For pastry decorations, trace shirt patterns onto tracing paper; cut out. Follow directions for crust to mix and roll out dough. Place patterns on dough and use a sharp knife to cut out. Refer to patterns and use a sharp knife to score detail lines on pocket, collar, and tie. Using dough scraps, shape small pieces of dough to resemble collar buttons. Cover and set aside.

Preheat oven to 425 degrees. For glaze, stir egg and milk together in a small bowl until well blended. Brush egg mixture evenly over top crust. Place shirt dough pieces on top crust. Place buttons on collar. Brush egg mixture over shirt dough pieces. Use a small paintbrush and red food coloring to paint diagonal stripes on tie. Cut slits in top of pie along edges of tie and pocket. Bake 40 to 45 minutes or until golden brown. Cool completely on a wire rack. Store in an airtight container.

Yield: 8 to 10 servings

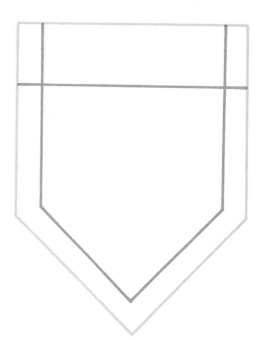

FATHER'S DAY INDULGENCE

On Father's Day, this gift will make it easy for Dad to relax! Sweet and crunchy Caramel-Coconut Corn is the perfect snack to serve him once he's settled in his favorite chair. When he's ready to watch the ball game or flip through the sports section, everything he needs will be right at his fingertips in this handy armchair caddy. Now that's luxury!

CARAMEL-COCONUT CORN

12 cups popped popcorn
3 cups dry-roasted peanuts
1 cup shredded sweetened coconut
1 cup firmly packed brown sugar
½ cup butter or margarine
¼ cup corn syrup
½ teaspoon salt
½ teaspoon baking soda
1 teaspoon coconut extract

In a very large bowl, combine popcorn, peanuts, and coconut.

Preheat oven to 200 degrees. Butter the sides of a large heavy saucepan. Combine sugar, butter, corn syrup, and salt in pan. Stirring constantly, cook over medium-low heat until sugar dissolves. Increase heat to medium and bring syrup to a boil. Cook, without stirring, 5 minutes. Remove from heat. Stir in baking soda (syrup will foam) and coconut extract. Pour syrup over popcorn mixture, stirring until well coated. Spoon mixture into two greased 9 x 13-inch baking pans. Bake 1 hour, stirring every 15 minutes. Cool completely in pans. Store in an airtight container.

Yield: about 18 cups caramel corn

ARMCHAIR CADDY

You will need the following pieces of fabric: two 8″ x 24″ pieces for caddy, two 7½″ x 8″ pieces for large pocket, two 4½″ x 8″ pieces for small pocket, and two 1½″ x 8″ bias strips and one 1½″ x 66″ bias strip for binding (pieced as necessary); paper-backed fusible web; lightweight fusible interfacing; and thread to match fabrics.

1. (*Note:* Follow Step 1 for each pair of caddy and pocket fabric pieces.) Follow manufacturers' instructions to fuse interfacing, then web, to wrong side of 1 fabric piece. Matching wrong sides and raw edges, fuse fabric pieces together.

2. For binding, match wrong sides and press each bias strip in half lengthwise; press long raw edges to center.

3. To bind each pocket, insert 1 long edge (top) of pocket between pressed edges of one 8″ length of binding; pin in place. Stitch all layers together close to inner edge of binding.

4. For pocket divider, match side and bottom edges and place small pocket on large pocket. Stitch through all layers from bottom edge to top edge of small pocket as shown in Fig. 1.

Fig. 1

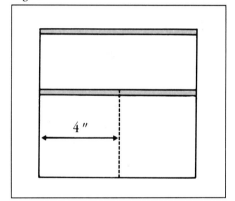

5. Matching bottom edge of pockets to 1 short edge (bottom) of caddy piece, place pockets on caddy. Baste all layers together along side and bottom edges of pockets.

6. To bind caddy, open 1 end of remaining binding length and press ¼″ to wrong side; refold binding. Beginning with unpressed end of binding, insert edges of caddy between long folded edges of binding; pin in place. Stitch all layers together close to inner edge of binding.

FIRST-CLASS PICNIC FARE

During *National
Picnic Month (July), supply
the provisions for a favorite
couple to enjoy an outdoor
adventure in eating! Crispy
vegetables and a tangy
dressing give Summer
Vegetable Salad its garden-
fresh goodness. Delectable
Salmon Sandwiches are a
savory departure from
traditional picnic fare.
Our watermelon pails
make cute carriers for the
food, napkins, and utensils.*

SUMMER VEGETABLE SALAD

    3 cups fresh broccoli flowerets
    3 cups shredded cabbage
    2 cups thinly sliced zucchini
 1 ½ cups sliced red onion
 1 ½ cups thinly sliced carrots
 1 ½ cups (about 6 ounces)
        shredded sharp Cheddar cheese
   ⅓ cup olive oil
   ⅓ cup buttermilk
   ¼ cup red wine vinegar
    1 teaspoon grainy mustard
    2 teaspoons salt
   ½ teaspoon ground black pepper
   ¼ teaspoon garlic powder

In a large bowl, combine vegetables
and cheese. In a medium bowl, whisk
together remaining ingredients. Pour oil
mixture over vegetables; toss until well
coated. Spoon into 1-pint jars and
screw on lids. Store in refrigerator.

Yield: about 10 cups salad

SALMON SANDWICHES

    1 package (8 ounces) cream cheese,
        softened
    1 teaspoon dried basil leaves,
        crushed
   ½ teaspoon garlic powder
      Salt
      Ground black pepper
      Garlic powder
    3 salmon steaks (about
        1 ½ pounds)
   ½ cup butter or margarine
   ¼ cup white wine
    1 bottle (3.5 ounces) capers
    4 large sandwich buns
      Cucumber slices

In a small bowl, stir together cream
cheese, basil, and ½ teaspoon garlic
powder; set aside.

Sprinkle salt, pepper, and garlic
powder evenly over both sides of
salmon. In a medium skillet, melt butter
over medium heat. Stir in wine and
capers. Add salmon, cover, and cook
10 minutes. Turn salmon, cover, and
cook 8 minutes longer or until flaky.
Remove from heat.

Spread cream cheese mixture evenly
over both halves of each bun. Reserving
butter mixture, place salmon on a
cutting board. Use a sharp knife to
remove skin and bones; cut into pieces
and place on bottom of each bun.
Spoon a small amount of reserved butter
mixture over salmon. Arrange cucumber
slices over salmon. Place top of each
bun over cucumber. Wrap sandwiches
individually in waxed paper. Store in
refrigerator.

Yield: 4 sandwiches

WATERMELON PAILS

For each pail, you will need a metal pail
(we found our 2-qt. pail at a paint
store); dk pink, green, dk green, and
black acrylic paint; glossy clear acrylic
spray; small pieces of cellulose sponge;
tagboard (manila folder); craft knife;
stencil brush; paper towels; cutting mat
or a thick layer of newspapers; graphite
transfer paper; tracing paper; removable
tape (optional); and masking tape.

1. Use masking tape to mask off handle
and rims of pail.
2. Dampen 1 sponge piece; wring out
excess water. Use sponge piece to stamp
inside of pail with dk pink paint; allow
to dry. Using another sponge piece and
green paint, repeat for outside of pail.
3. Cut an approx. 1"w piece from
sponge. Use sponge piece and dk green
paint to stamp vertical stripes approx.
1" apart around outside of pail; allow
to dry.
4. Follow Stenciling, page 122, to
stencil black seeds on inside of pail.
5. Allowing to dry between coats, apply
several coats of acrylic spray to inside
and outside of pail. Remove masking
tape.

SEED

"WEENIE DOG" BASKET

We double-dog dare you to find anything better to give to your favorite picnickers than our Italian Mustard and Sweet Pickle Relish! These gourmet condiments are sure to add zip to hot dogs and hamburgers. Both are tucked inside our ''weenie dog'' basket, which can hold lots of knickknacks or treats long after the Dog Days of summer are over.

ITALIAN MUSTARD

¾ cup prepared yellow mustard
2 tablespoons dried minced onion
2 tablespoons chopped fresh chives
1 tablespoon garlic powder
1 teaspoon dried oregano leaves

In a small bowl, stir together all ingredients. Transfer to an airtight container and refrigerate 8 hours or overnight to allow flavors to blend. Store in refrigerator.

Yield: about ¾ cup mustard

SWEET PICKLE RELISH

1 jar (32 ounces) kosher dill pickles, drained and rinsed
1 tablespoon vegetable oil
¼ cup finely chopped celery
2 tablespoons finely chopped onion
¼ cup red wine vinegar
3 tablespoons granulated sugar
3 tablespoons honey

In a blender or food processor, finely chop pickles. Transfer to a medium bowl.

In a small skillet, heat oil over medium heat. Add celery and onion; cook until tender. Add celery mixture and remaining ingredients to pickles, stirring until sugar dissolves. Transfer to an airtight container and refrigerate 8 hours or overnight to allow flavors to blend. Store in refrigerator.

Yield: about 3 cups relish

''WEENIE DOG'' BASKET

You will need a 4"w x 12"l x 3"h basket; the following pieces of brown fabric: two 6" squares for head, two 5" x 19" pieces for legs, four 4" x 5" pieces for feet, four 4" x 6" pieces for ears, and one 4" x 10" piece for tail; fabric to line basket; brown thread; heavy black thread (buttonhole twist); black embroidery floss; one 1" dia. plastic foam ball; polyester fiberfill; one ½" dia. black button for nose; two ⅛" dia. black doll buttons for eyes; black and red permanent felt-tip pens with fine points; fabric marking pencil; tracing paper; hot glue gun; and glue sticks.

1. Use head, legs, foot, and ear patterns, page 117, and follow Tracing Patterns and Sewing Shapes, page 122, to make head, legs, 2 feet, and 2 ears from fabric pieces.

2. For head, stuff head half full with fiberfill. For muzzle, place foam ball inside head against center of 1 fabric piece. Finish stuffing head, keeping ball in place. Sew final closure by hand.

3. For nose, sew ½" dia. button over plastic foam ball.

4. For each eye, use heavy thread and come up through head. Thread needle through one ⅛" dia. button and go down through head approx. ⅛" away. Pull thread tightly to create a dimple in head. Repeat to make several stitches. Knot thread and trim ends.

5. Use black pen to draw mouth and tongue outline. Use red pen to color tongue.

6. For ears, sew final closure by hand. For tuck at base of each ear, refer to pattern and fold ear along solid line. Match fold to dotted line; tack in place. Whipstitch ears to head at seamline.

7. Stuff legs and feet with fiberfill; sew final closures by hand. For toes, use 3 strands of floss and bring needle through foot at one ●, over top of foot, and back through foot, coming out at same ●; pull floss tight. Knot and secure floss ends. Repeat for remaining ●'s.

8. For tail, trace pattern, page 117, onto tracing paper; cut out. Cut 1 tail from 4" x 10" fabric piece. Matching wrong sides and long edges, fold tail in half. Using a ¼" seam allowance, sew long edges together. Turn right side out. Stuff with fiberfill; sew final closure by hand.

9. To assemble basket, glue feet to 1 end of basket; glue tail to bottom of basket between feet. Glue legs and head to opposite end of basket. Line basket with fabric.

UNCLE SAM'S SNACK MIX

*U*ncle Sam wants you to help a friend have a great Fourth of July. And this zesty Fiesta Snack Mix is just the way to do it! Flavored with taco seasoning and Parmesan cheese, the mix is a tasty snack to take along to a picnic or fireworks display. Great for delivering the treat, the Uncle Sam canister also makes a cute decoration for the day.

FIESTA SNACK MIX

1 can (7½ ounces) corn chips
1 can (12 ounces) mixed salted nuts
¼ cup butter or margarine, melted
¼ cup grated Parmesan cheese
2 teaspoons taco seasoning mix

Preheat oven to 325 degrees. In a large bowl, combine corn chips and nuts. In a small bowl, combine butter, cheese, and taco seasoning mix. Pour over corn chip mixture. Stir until well coated. Spread mixture evenly on a baking sheet. Bake 12 minutes. Cool completely. Store in an airtight container.

Yield: about 6 cups snack mix

UNCLE SAM CANISTER

You will need one 7"h x 4" dia. cardboard snack chip canister (we used a 7½ ounce corn chip can); blue, white, peach, red, black, lt blue, pink, and silver acrylic paint; red and matte white spray paint; modeling paste (available at art supply stores); two 1¼" lengths of ⅜"w gold braid trim; three ½"w gold gummed stars; graphite transfer paper; tracing paper; paintbrushes; and craft glue.

1. (*Note:* Allow to dry after each paint color.) Spray paint canister white and lid red.
2. Use acrylic paint to paint a ⅛"w red line around canister 1⅝" below top edge.
3. For hat stripes, paint ⅜"w blue stripes ⅜" apart around top of canister.
4. For trousers, paint bottom 1" of canister (including rim) blue. For stripes on sides of trousers, paint a ½"w vertical white stripe on each side of canister; paint a ⅛"w vertical red stripe in center of each white stripe.
5. For shoes, paint 2 black semicircles on front of canister approx. 2" apart.
6. For belt, paint a ⅜"w black band around canister above trousers. Paint silver belt buckle on belt.
7. Trace Uncle Sam pattern, page 118, onto tracing paper. Center pattern on canister over white area; use transfer paper to transfer pattern to canister.
8. Use a paintbrush to apply modeling paste to canister to form eyebrows, mustache, beard, and hair around face and on back of canister; allow to dry.
9. Paint face and hands peach, eyes blue with white highlights, mouth red, cheeks pink, and outlines of eyes and nose black.
10. Paint brim of hat red. Paint sleeve and collar outlines lt blue.
11. For epaulets, glue 1 length of gold trim over top of each shoulder. Apply gold stars to hat brim.

STAR-SPANGLED COOKIES

*F*riends will get a bang out of these patriotic cookies for the Fourth of July. The "firecrackers" are made from purchased wafer roll cookies, and the Stenciled Star Cookies have a rich maple flavor. A flag-toting basket makes a spirited gift container.

FIRECRACKER COOKIES

COOKIES

- 12 ounces vanilla-flavored almond bark
- 2 dozen purchased wafer roll cookies, such as Pepperidge Farms® Pirouette cookies
- 24 pieces (2 inches each) red string licorice

ICING

- 2⅔ cups sifted confectioners sugar
- 2 egg whites
- Red and blue paste food coloring

For cookies, melt almond bark in a small saucepan over low heat, stirring constantly. Remove from heat. Using a fork, dip each cookie into almond bark, coating completely. Transfer to a wire rack with waxed paper underneath. Before almond bark hardens, insert 1 piece of licorice into 1 end of each cookie. Allow almond bark to harden.

For icing, beat sugar and egg whites in a medium bowl 7 to 10 minutes or until stiff. Divide icing into 2 bowls; tint red and blue. Transfer each icing to a separate pastry bag fitted with a very small round tip. Refer to photo and pipe icing on each cookie. Allow icing to harden. Store in an airtight container.

Yield: 2 dozen cookies

STENCILED STAR COOKIES

- 1 cup butter or margarine, softened
- 2 cups firmly packed brown sugar
- 2 eggs
- 1 teaspoon maple flavoring
- 3½ cups all-purpose flour
- 1 teaspoon baking soda
- ½ teaspoon salt
- 1 cup sliced almonds, chopped
- Red liquid food coloring

In a large bowl, cream butter and sugar until fluffy. Add eggs and maple flavoring; beat until smooth. In a medium bowl, stir together flour, baking soda, and salt. Add flour mixture to creamed mixture; stir until a soft dough forms. Stir in almonds. Cover and chill 1 hour.

Preheat oven to 375 degrees. On a lightly floured surface, use a floured rolling pin to roll out dough to ¼-inch thickness. Use a 3-inch round cookie cutter to cut out cookies. Transfer to a greased baking sheet. Bake 8 to 10 minutes or until edges begin to brown. Transfer to a wire rack to cool completely.

Using star pattern and food coloring, follow Stenciling, page 122, to stencil stars on cookies. Store in an airtight container.

Yield: about 3½ dozen cookies

EVERYBODY LOVES A CLOWN

Everybody loves a clown! Our cuddly doll makes a cute gift for International Clown Week (celebrated annually August 1-7). And since clowns and circuses go hand in hand, we included a batch of homemade Animal Cookies.

ANIMAL COOKIES

COOKIES

1⅔ cups butter, softened
¾ cup sifted confectioners sugar
1 teaspoon vanilla extract
1 teaspoon almond extract
2⅔ cups all-purpose flour

ICING

2 cups sifted confectioners sugar
6 tablespoons milk

For cookies, preheat oven to 375 degrees. In a large bowl, cream butter and sugar until fluffy. Add extracts; beat until smooth. Stir in flour. On a lightly floured surface, use a floured rolling pin to roll out dough to ¼-inch thickness. Use an animal-shaped cookie cutter to cut out cookies. Transfer to a greased baking sheet. Bake 8 to 10 minutes or until edges are light brown. Transfer to a wire rack with waxed paper underneath to cool completely.

For icing, stir together sugar and milk in a small bowl until smooth. Ice cookies. Allow icing to harden. Store in an airtight container.

Yield: about 3 dozen 3-inch cookies

SOCK CLOWN

You will need 1 men's white crew sock; 3" dia. red felt doll's hat, orange curly doll hair, and 4" plastic clown boots (available at craft stores); one ½" dia. red pom-pom; two 1" dia. green pom-poms; red, yellow, and black felt; two 7½" x 8" fabric pieces for arms; one 4" x 14" reversible fabric piece for collar; two 1½" x 9½" reversible fabric pieces for leg ruffles; white and yellow thread; thread to match fabrics; baby rickrack to match fabrics; white paint pen with fine point; polyester fiberfill; removable fabric marking pen;

hot glue gun; glue sticks; tracing paper; and fabric glue.

1. For head, stuff 3½" of sock toe with fiberfill. Using several strands of thread, wrap thread tightly around sock below fiberfill; knot thread and trim ends. Stuff remainder of sock foot with fiberfill.

2. For legs, place sock, heel side down, on a flat surface; flatten sock ribbing. Trim ribbing to 7" long. Use fabric marking pen to draw a line down center of ribbing. Cutting through both layers of ribbing, cut along drawn line. Using a double strand of thread and turning raw edges under slightly, whipstitch cut edges of ribbing together to form legs. Stuff legs with fiberfill. Fold leg openings ½" to wrong side. Insert 1 boot into each leg opening; hot glue to secure.

3. (*Note:* Use a ¼" seam allowance throughout.) For each leg ruffle, use fabric glue to glue a 9½" length of rickrack along 1 long edge of one 1½" x 9½" fabric piece; allow to dry. Matching right sides and short edges, fold fabric in half; sew short edges together. Turn right side out. Press remaining raw edge ¼" to wrong side; baste along pressed edge. Place ruffle over end of leg. Pull basting thread, drawing up gathers to fit leg. Knot thread and trim ends.

4. Trace patterns onto tracing paper; cut out. Use patterns to cut 4 hand pieces from yellow felt, 2 eyes from black felt, and 1 mouth from red felt. Use paint pen to paint a white line along center of mouth.

5. For each hand, use fabric glue to glue a cotton ball-sized piece of fiberfill to palm of 1 hand piece. Place a second hand piece over fiberfill; glue edges of hand pieces together. Using yellow

thread, stitch where indicated by dotted lines on pattern to form fingers.

6. For each arm, use fabric glue to glue an 8" length of rickrack along 1 long edge of one 7½" x 8" fabric piece; allow to dry. Matching right sides and short edges, fold fabric in half. Sew short edges together to form a tube. Turn right side out. Press remaining raw edge ¼" to wrong side; baste along pressed edge. Pull basting thread tightly to close top of tube. Knot thread and trim ends. Lightly stuff tube with fiberfill to 1" from opening.

7. Insert top of 1 hand 1½" into 1 arm. Wrap thread tightly around arm and hand 1" from bottom edge of arm to secure; knot thread and trim ends. Tack top of arm to side of clown at neck. Repeat for remaining arm.

8. For collar, match right sides and short edges and fold 4" x 14" fabric piece in half; sew short edges together to form a tube. Matching wrong sides and raw edges, press tube in half. Baste along pressed edge. Use fabric glue to glue rickrack along each raw edge of collar; allow to dry. Place collar around neck. Pull basting thread, drawing up gathers to fit neck. Knot thread and trim ends.

9. Cut two 8" bunches of hair; knot center of each bunch. Hot glue knot of 1 bunch to each side of head. Trim hair as desired.

10. Hot glue hat to head.

11. Use fabric glue to glue eyes, red pom-pom, and mouth to head. Glue green pom-poms to body. Allow to dry.

LEISURE-TIME COOKIE BASKET

*O*n *Labor Day, a friend will enjoy these Peanut Butter Potato Chip Cookies while she relaxes with a favorite pastime such as sewing, gardening, cooking, or painting. To dress up your basket, create a keepsake hobby pin by decorating a wooden heart with miniatures reflecting her special interest.*

PEANUT BUTTER POTATO CHIP COOKIES

- 1¼ cups butter or margarine, softened
- 1 cup firmly packed brown sugar
- ½ cup granulated sugar
- 2 eggs
- 1 teaspoon vanilla extract
- 2¾ cups all-purpose flour
- 1 package (12 ounces) peanut butter chips
- 1 bag (7 ounces) rippled potato chips, coarsely crushed

Preheat oven to 350 degrees. In a large bowl, cream butter and sugars until fluffy. Add eggs and vanilla; beat until smooth. Add flour; stir until a soft dough forms. Stir in peanut butter chips and potato chips. Drop batter by tablespoonfuls 1-inch apart onto a greased baking sheet. Bake 10 to 12 minutes or until edges are light brown. Transfer to a wire rack to cool completely. Store in an airtight container.

Yield: about 8 dozen cookies

HOBBY PINS

For each pin, you will need a heart-shaped wooden cutout, items to decorate cutout (we used miniatures, fabric, and paint), pin back, matte Mod Podge® sealer, foam brush, high gloss clear epoxy coating (we used Aristocrat™ Epoxy Thick Crystal Clear Coating), hot glue gun, and glue sticks.

1. Decorate cutout as desired, using Mod Podge® sealer to secure items. Allow to dry.

2. Allowing to dry between coats, apply 2 coats of Mod Podge® sealer to cutout, including sides and back of cutout.
3. (*Note:* Read all epoxy coating instructions before beginning.) Apply coating to front of cutout; allow to dry.
4. Hot glue pin back to back of cutout.

A NEIGHBORLY OFFERING

*O*n *National Good Neighbor Day (the fourth Sunday in September), show your appreciation for a great neighbor with this friendly gift. A delicious addition to muffins, sweet and fruity Pineapple-Ginger Jam makes breakfast an extra-special occasion! To deliver your neighborly offering, tuck a jar of the jam in a little basket spruced up with cheerful flowers and a bow.*

PINEAPPLE-GINGER JAM

  1 jar (12 ounces) pineapple
     jam or preserves
  1 tablespoon crème de cacao
     liqueur
  ¼ teaspoon ground ginger

In a small bowl, combine all ingredients, stirring until well blended. Spoon jam into an airtight container. Refrigerate 8 hours or overnight to allow flavors to blend. Store in refrigerator.

Yield: about 1 cup jam

NEIGHBOR BASKETS

For each basket, you will need a jar with lid, basket to hold jar, fabric to cover jar lid, ¼"w satin and grosgrain ribbons, artificial flowers, wood excelsior, paper for tag, felt-tip pen with fine point, fabric marking pencil, craft glue, hot glue gun, and glue sticks.

1. To cover jar lid, use fabric marking pencil to draw around jar lid on wrong side of fabric; cut out fabric ¼" outside pencil line. Clip edges of fabric at ½" intervals to within ⅛" of pencil line. Center fabric on jar lid. Pulling fabric taut, use craft glue to glue clipped edges to side of lid. Hot glue grosgrain ribbon around side of lid.
2. Tie lengths of satin and grosgrain ribbons together into a bow. Hot glue bow and flowers to basket. Line basket with excelsior. Place jar in basket.
3. For tag, cut a rectangle from paper and write "To A <u>Great</u> Neighbor!" on tag with pen. Hot glue tag to basket.

OLD-FASHIONED APPLE CAKES

A basketful of these spicy Apple Cakes makes a wonderful remembrance for National Grandparents Day (the first Sunday in September after Labor Day). To make the gift extra special, our mugs feature cross-stitched inserts with places for photographs of Grandma and Grandpa's little angels.

APPLE CAKES

2¼ cups all-purpose flour
¾ teaspoon baking powder
½ teaspoon plus ⅛ teaspoon
    ground cinnamon, divided
¼ teaspoon salt
¼ teaspoon ground allspice
¼ teaspoon ground nutmeg
¼ cup butter or margarine, softened
¾ cup plus 2 tablespoons granulated
    sugar, divided
3 eggs
½ cup vegetable oil
1 tablespoon vanilla extract
2 cups peeled, cored, and chopped
    Granny Smith apples (reserve
    peel from 1 apple)
½ cup chopped walnuts

Preheat oven to 400 degrees. In a medium bowl, stir together flour, baking powder, ½ teaspoon cinnamon, salt, allspice, and nutmeg. In a large bowl, cream butter and ¾ cup sugar until fluffy. Add eggs, oil, and vanilla; stir until smooth. Add dry ingredients to creamed mixture; stir until well blended. Finely chop reserved apple peel. Stir in apples, apple peel, and walnuts. Spoon batter into paper-lined muffin pan, filling each tin ¾ full. Bake 15 to 18 minutes or until a toothpick inserted in center of cake comes out clean. Transfer to a wire rack. In a small bowl, stir together remaining sugar and cinnamon. Sprinkle tops of warm cakes with sugar mixture. Cool completely. Store in an airtight container.

Yield: about 1½ dozen cakes

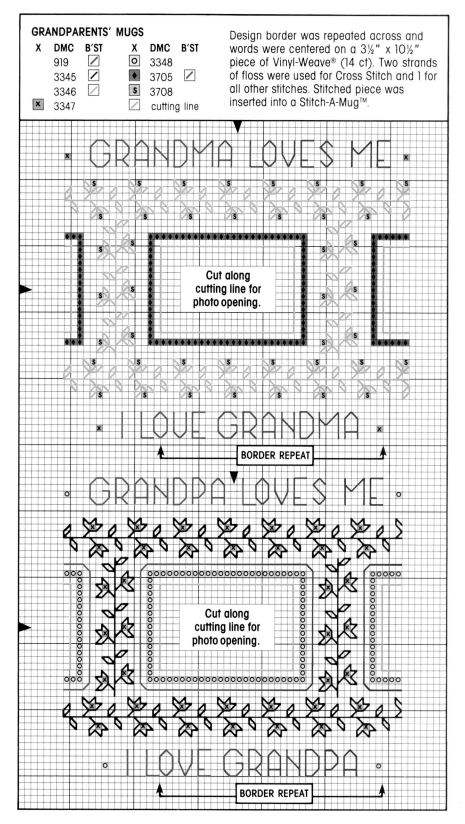

GRANDPARENTS' MUGS

X	DMC	B'ST		X	DMC	B'ST
	919	╱		○	3348	
	3345	╱		◆	3705	╱
	3346	╱		S	3708	
☒	3347					cutting line ╱

Design border was repeated across and words were centered on a 3½" x 10½" piece of Vinyl-Weave® (14 ct). Two strands of floss were used for Cross Stitch and 1 for all other stitches. Stitched piece was inserted into a Stitch-A-Mug™.

GRANDMA LOVES ME

Cut along cutting line for photo opening.

I LOVE GRANDMA

BORDER REPEAT

GRANDPA LOVES ME

Cut along cutting line for photo opening.

I LOVE GRANDPA

BORDER REPEAT

BREAKFAST BLUEBERRIES

Columbus would have loved this breakfast treat while sailing the ocean blue! Bursting with plump blueberries, our tasty jam is a cute gift for Columbus Day (the second Monday in October). It's wonderful with toast or cream cheese and bagels. To help a friend chart new territory, present a jar of the jam in a clever gift bag created with ''Old World'' wrapping paper.

BLUEBERRY JAM

2 cups frozen unsweetened
   blueberries, thawed and
   drained
1 box (1¾ ounces) pectin
4 cups granulated sugar

In a large saucepan or Dutch oven, combine blueberries and pectin over medium-high heat. Stirring constantly, bring to a rolling boil; cook until pectin dissolves. Stirring constantly, add sugar and bring to a rolling boil again; boil 1 minute longer. Remove from heat; skim off foam. Store in an airtight container in refrigerator or follow Canning Instructions, page 124, processing in boiling water bath 15 minutes.

Yield: about 2 pints jam

GIFT SACK

You will need wrapping paper, a button, thread to match button, cotton string, ⅛″ hole punch, glue stick, and masking tape.

1. (*Note:* Refer to Fig. 1 for Step 1.) For sack, cut a 13″ x 17½″ piece of wrapping paper. Fold 1 long edge (top) of paper ½″ to wrong side; glue to secure. Unfolding paper after each fold, fold 1 short edge 2¾″ to wrong side, 4⅜″ to right side, 6″ and 11¼″ to wrong side, 12⅞″ to right side, and 14½″ to wrong side. Fold bottom edge of paper 1⅞″ to wrong side (Fold A); unfold. Mark a dot where Fold A intersects 4⅜″ fold and 12⅞″ fold. Overlapping edges ½″, glue short edges of paper together to form sack shape.

Fig. 1

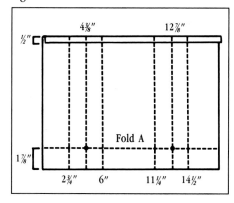

2. For bottom of sack, flatten sack along vertical folds with 4⅜″ and 12⅞″ folds to inside of flattened sack (Fig. 2a). Refer to Fig. 2a to fold bottom of sack up 3½″. Open bottom of sack below 3½″ fold and grasp sack, placing thumbs over dots inside sack. Referring to Fig. 2b, push dots outward with thumbs and match dots to outer folded edges of sack, forming a box. Fold side flaps to inside of box shape, flattening bottom of sack (Fig. 2c). Fold bottom up (Fig. 2d) and top down (Fig. 2e). Glue flaps together. Open sack.

Fig. 2a

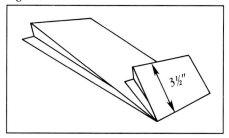

Fig. 2b

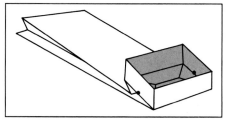

Fig. 2c

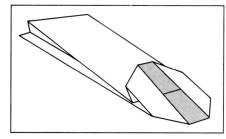

Fig. 2d

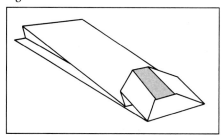

Fig. 2e

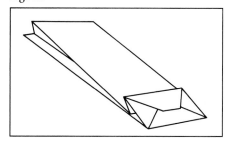

3. For button closure, place sack with seam at center back. Place a small piece of tape inside center front of sack 4½″ below top of sack. Sew button to sack through tape. Place a small piece of tape inside center back of sack ½″ below top of sack. Punch a hole in sack through tape. Thread string through hole; knot each end of string. Fold top of sack 1½″ to front; wrap string around button.

COFFEE LOVER'S BASKET

A coffee lover will appreciate this fine gift, especially during Gourmet Coffee Week (celebrated annually October 15-21). The elegant basket features a jar of Mocha Sugar, which can be used to add rich flavor and a hint of cinnamon to coffee, espresso, or cappuccino. A lace handkerchief makes a nice wrapper for a bag of fresh-roasted coffee beans. A handsome pair of cups and saucers completes the gift.

MOCHA SUGAR

1¼ cups granulated sugar
3 tablespoons coffee-flavored
   liqueur
½ teaspoon ground cinnamon

In a small bowl, stir all ingredients together until well blended. Store in an airtight container. Give with serving suggestion.

Yield: about 1 cup sugar

To serve: Stir desired amount of sugar into coffee.

COFFEE BASKET

You will need a white basket; jar with lid; silver, white, and green ribbons; silver angel hair; silver berry spray; silver spray paint; handkerchief; silver cord; white and silver paper; green calligraphy pen; hot glue gun; glue sticks; and spray adhesive.

1. For basket, tie ribbon lengths together into a bow; knot streamers at desired intervals. Hot glue bow and streamers to basket. Line basket with angel hair.
2. For jar, spray paint outside of jar lid silver; allow to dry. Hot glue berry spray around jar.
3. For jar label, use pen to write "MOCHA SUGAR" on white paper; cut label desired size. Use spray adhesive to apply label to silver paper; trim silver paper ⅛" from label. Use spray adhesive to apply label to jar.
4. For coffee bundle, place a plastic bag of coffee beans in center of handkerchief. Gather corners of handkerchief together; tie cord around handkerchief to secure. For tag, use pen to write "COFFEE" on white paper; cut paper into tag shape. Make a hole in pointed end of tag. Thread tag onto 1 end of cord; tie cord into a bow. Knot ends of cord.

INCREDIBLY DELICIOUS PIE

*O*n *Sweetest Day (the third Saturday in October), surprise a friend with this incredibly delicious Coconut-Chocolate Meringue Pie. The luscious dessert features creamy coconut custard swirled with chocolate. What a sweet surprise!*

COCONUT-CHOCOLATE MERINGUE PIE

CRUST

    1½ cups all-purpose flour
    ½   teaspoon salt
    ½   cup vegetable shortening
    ¼   cup cold water

FILLING

    ¾   cup granulated sugar
    ⅓   cup all-purpose flour
    ¼   teaspoon salt
    1   cup milk
    1   cup half and half
    3   egg yolks, beaten
    2   tablespoons butter or margarine
    1   teaspoon vanilla extract
    1   teaspoon coconut extract
    1   cup sweetened shredded coconut
    1   package (6 ounces) semisweet
          chocolate chips

MERINGUE

    3   egg whites
    ¼   teaspoon coconut extract
    ¼   teaspoon cream of tartar
    6   tablespoons sifted confectioners
          sugar
    ¼   cup sweetened shredded coconut

For crust, preheat oven to 450 degrees. In a medium bowl, stir together flour and salt. Using a pastry blender or 2 knives, cut in shortening until mixture resembles coarse meal. Sprinkle with water; mix until a soft dough forms. On a lightly floured surface, use a floured rolling pin to roll out dough to ⅛-inch thickness. Transfer to a 9-inch pie plate and use a sharp knife to trim edge of dough. Prick bottom of crust with a fork. Bake 10 to 12 minutes or until light brown. Cool completely on a wire rack.

For filling, combine sugar, flour, and salt in a medium saucepan. Gradually stir in milk and half and half. Stirring constantly, cook over medium heat until mixture begins to boil. Remove from heat. Place egg yolks in a small bowl. Add about ½ cup milk mixture to egg yolks; stir until well blended. Gradually add egg yolk mixture to milk mixture in saucepan, stirring until well blended. Return to heat and bring to a boil. Stirring constantly, cook 2 to 3 minutes or until mixture begins to thicken and coats the back of a spoon. Remove from heat. Add butter and extracts. Stir in coconut. Pour custard mixture into cooled crust. Stirring constantly, melt chocolate chips in a small saucepan over low heat. Pour chocolate over custard mixture and swirl with a knife.

For meringue, preheat oven to 350 degrees. In a medium bowl, beat first three ingredients until soft peaks form. Gradually add sugar, beating until stiff. Spread meringue over filling, sealing to edge of pastry. Sprinkle coconut over meringue. Bake 12 to 15 minutes or until meringue is light brown. Cover and store in refrigerator.

Yield: 8 to 10 servings

OFFICE PICNIC

*O*n National Boss
Day (October 16), treat a
busy boss to a ready-to-eat
box lunch! Delicious cold,
Oven-Fried Chicken features
a zesty herbed breading. A
favorite with fried chicken,
our Extra-Special Potato
Salad gets a bit of crunch
from chopped radishes. For
a presentation that's sure
to merit a commendation,
pack this "picnic" in our
cute briefcase made from
a cardboard mailing box.

EXTRA-SPECIAL POTATO SALAD

$3\frac{1}{2}$ pounds red potatoes (about
    7 large potatoes)
  6 hard-cooked eggs, chopped
  8 slices bacon, cooked, drained,
    and crumbled
  $\frac{1}{2}$ cup chopped radishes
  $\frac{1}{2}$ cup chopped green onion
  $\frac{1}{2}$ cup finely chopped fresh parsley
  $\frac{1}{4}$ cup chopped green pepper
  1 cup sour cream
  $\frac{1}{2}$ cup mayonnaise
  2 tablespoons Dijon-style mustard
  1 teaspoon salt
  1 teaspoon ground black pepper
  $\frac{1}{2}$ teaspoon dried dill weed

In a large Dutch oven, cover potatoes
with salted water. Bring water to a boil
and cook until potatoes are tender.
Drain potatoes and cool completely.
Peel and dice potatoes. In a large

bowl, stir together potatoes and next
6 ingredients. In a medium bowl, stir
together remaining ingredients. Pour
sour cream mixture over potato mixture
and stir until well blended. Cover and
refrigerate until ready to serve.
Yield: about 10 cups potato salad

OVEN-FRIED CHICKEN

  2 pounds boneless skinless chicken
    breast fillets
    Salt and ground black pepper
  $1\frac{1}{2}$ cups plain nonfat yogurt
  $\frac{1}{2}$ cup grated Parmesan cheese
  1 teaspoon paprika
  1 teaspoon dried thyme leaves
  $\frac{1}{2}$ teaspoon garlic powder
  $1\frac{1}{2}$ cups plain bread crumbs
  3 tablespoons butter or margarine,
    melted

Preheat oven to 400 degrees.
Sprinkle chicken with salt and pepper.
In a small bowl, whisk yogurt, cheese,
paprika, thyme, and garlic powder. In
another small bowl, stir together bread
crumbs and butter. Dip chicken, one
piece at a time, into yogurt mixture,
then place in bread crumb mixture.
Spoon bread crumb mixture over
chicken, coating well. Place coated
pieces of chicken in a greased baking
pan. Bake 25 to 30 minutes or until
juices run clear when thickest part of
chicken is pierced with a fork. Cover
and refrigerate until ready to present.
Serve cold.

Yield: about 6 servings

BRIEFCASE LUNCH BOX

You will need one $11\frac{1}{4}$" x $8\frac{5}{8}$" x 4"
mailing box, heavy grey paper, black
felt-tip pen with fine point, black paper,
white poster board, silver cord, tracing
paper, graphite transfer paper, spray
adhesive, craft glue, $\frac{1}{8}$" hole punch,
and craft knife.

1. For briefcase, follow Gift Box 2
instructions, page 123, to cover box
with grey paper.
2. Use patterns and follow Tracing
Patterns, page 122; do not cut out
buckle pattern. Use handle pattern to
cut 1 handle from grey paper. Use
transfer paper to transfer buckle pattern
to grey paper; cut out buckle.
3. Use black pen to draw detail lines on
briefcase, handle, and buckle and to
color in holes on buckle.
4. Fold ends of handle 1" to wrong
side. Use craft glue to glue buckle and
folded ends of handle to briefcase.
5. For tag, draw a tag shape on black
paper; draw a line $\frac{1}{4}$" inside first line.
Cut out along drawn lines. Use spray
adhesive to apply paper to poster
board. Trim poster board even with
outside edge of paper. Use black pen to
write "TO A GREAT BOSS!" on tag.
Punch a hole in point of tag. Thread tag
onto cord. Tie cord to handle.

CELEBRATION BREAD

*D*ecked out with colorful little flags from around the world, this loaf of Braided Cornmeal Bread honors United Nations Day (October 24). Delicious served warm with butter, the yeast bread gets its hearty flavor from molasses and cornmeal. To make your gift even more memorable, present the loaf on a handsome breadboard.

BRAIDED CORNMEAL BREAD

2½ cups water
½ cup yellow cornmeal
1 teaspoon salt
½ cup molasses
2 tablespoons vegetable shortening
2 packages dry yeast
½ cup warm water
5¾ cups all-purpose flour
   Vegetable cooking spray

In a medium saucepan, combine 2½ cups water, cornmeal, and salt. Stirring frequently, bring cornmeal mixture to a boil. Reduce heat to medium-low; cook 5 minutes. Remove from heat; stir in molasses and shortening. Cool to room temperature.

In a small bowl, dissolve yeast in ½ cup warm water. In a large bowl, stir together cornmeal mixture and yeast mixture. Gradually stir in flour. Turn dough onto a lightly floured surface and knead until dough becomes smooth and elastic. Place in a large bowl sprayed with cooking spray, turning once to coat top of dough. Cover and let rise in a warm place (80 to 85 degrees) 1 hour or until doubled in size. Turn dough onto a lightly floured surface and punch down. Divide dough in half. Use a floured rolling pin to roll one-half of dough into a 9 x 13-inch rectangle. Cut rectangle lengthwise into 3 equal strips. Braid strips; transfer to a greased baking sheet. Join ends of dough to form a circle. Spray top of dough with cooking spray. Repeat for remaining dough. Cover and let rise in a warm place 1 hour or until doubled in size.

Preheat oven to 375 degrees. Bake 25 to 30 minutes or until golden brown and bread sounds hollow when tapped. Transfer to a wire rack to cool completely. Store in an airtight container.

Yield: 2 loaves bread

FOR A SPECIAL LADY

*O*n Mother-in-Law Day (the fourth Sunday in October), surprise this special lady with buttery Toffee Cookies. The chewy cookies feature crisp bits of chocolate-covered English toffee. To dress up your gift basket, add a pretty padded lid — she'll enjoy using it long after the cookies are gone.

TOFFEE COOKIES

   1 cup butter or margarine, softened
   ¾ cup granulated sugar
   ¾ cup firmly packed brown sugar
   2 eggs
   1 tablespoon vanilla extract
2¼ cups all-purpose flour
   1 teaspoon baking soda
   1 teaspoon salt
   2 cups coarsely chopped chocolate-covered English toffee bars

Preheat oven to 350 degrees. In a large bowl, cream butter and sugars until fluffy. Add eggs and vanilla; beat until smooth. In a medium bowl, stir together flour, baking soda, and salt. Add dry ingredients to creamed mixture; stir until a soft dough forms. Stir in toffee bars. Drop by heaping tablespoonfuls 2 inches apart onto a greased baking sheet. Bake 8 to 10 minutes or until edges are light brown. Transfer to a wire rack to cool completely. Store in an airtight container.

Yield: about 6½ dozen cookies

PADDED BASKET LID

You will need a basket, fabric, pregathered eyelet trim, purchased cording, two 24″ lengths of satin ribbon, medium weight cardboard, polyester bonded batting, and craft glue.

1. Measure length and width of basket opening. Cut 2 pieces of cardboard and 2 pieces of batting the determined measurements. Cut 2 pieces of fabric 1″ larger on all sides than cardboard.
2. (*Note:* Allow to dry after each glue step.) For lid top, center both pieces of batting, then 1 cardboard piece, on wrong side of 1 fabric piece. At ½″ intervals, clip edges of fabric piece to ⅛″ from edge of cardboard. Pulling fabric taut, glue clipped edges of fabric to wrong side of cardboard.

3. For trim, measure around lid top; add 1″. Cut 1 length each of cording and eyelet trim the determined measurement. Glue cording, then eyelet trim, to wrong side of lid top. For ties, fold each ribbon length in half. On wrong side of lid top, glue 1″ of 1 folded ribbon end to center of 1 edge of lid top. Repeat to glue remaining folded ribbon end to opposite edge of lid top.
4. For lid bottom, repeat Step 2 (omitting batting) to cover remaining cardboard piece.
5. Matching wrong sides, glue lid top and bottom together. Place lid on basket. Thread ribbon ends through basket. Tie ribbons into bows; trim ends.

HAUNTING HALLOWEEN PIZZA

*T*his Chocolate Pizza is a hauntingly good treat for Halloween. The "crust" is made of chocolate and peanuts, and candy corn makes a colorful topping. For a spooky delivery, pack the pizza in a carryout box from the "Haunted House of Pizza."

CHOCOLATE PIZZA

1 package (12 ounces) semisweet chocolate chips
1 cup roasted peanuts
1 cup candy corn

Line a 9-inch round cake pan with plastic wrap. Stirring constantly, melt chocolate chips in a medium saucepan over low heat. Remove from heat; stir in peanuts. Pour into pan. To decorate, press candy corn into chocolate mixture. Cool completely at room temperature. Remove from pan. Peel away plastic wrap. Store in an airtight container at room temperature. Cut into wedges to serve.

Yield: 10 to 12 servings

HALLOWEEN PIZZA BOX

You will need a small pizza carryout box (ours measures 9½" x 9½" x 2"); brown craft paper; one 10" square each of orange, purple, and black construction paper; white paper; graphite transfer paper; grey, neon yellow, neon green, lt brown, brown, white, and silver colored pencils; black felt-tip pen with fine point; brown, orange, and yellow felt-tip markers; ½"h black vinyl stick-on letters (available at craft or art supply stores); 1⅜"w craft ribbon; tracing paper; spray adhesive; large paper clips; and craft glue.

Note: Use spray adhesive for all gluing unless otherwise indicated.

1. To cover box lid, cut a piece of craft paper same size as box lid; glue paper to lid.
2. Use arch, window, ghost, and bat patterns, page 119, and follow Tracing Patterns, page 122; do not cut out ghost and window patterns.
3. Use arch pattern to cut arch from purple paper. Center arch pattern over black paper; draw around arch opening. Trim black paper ¼" outside drawn line.
4. With bottom of window pattern even with bottom of black paper, use transfer paper to transfer window to center of black paper.
5. Use brown and lt brown pencils to color window frame; use white pencil to color broken window panes. Center purple arch over black paper; secure with paper clips. Use grey pencil to draw stones around window. Remove paper clips and arch.
6. For ghost, use transfer paper to transfer ghost to white paper. Draw over transferred lines with black pen. Use silver pencil and brown, orange, and yellow felt-tip markers to color pizza pan and pizza. Cut out ghost.
7. With bottom of ghost even with bottom of black paper, glue ghost over window design. Use neon yellow and neon green pencils to draw spooky eyes around ghost.
8. Glue black paper to orange paper. Glue purple arch over black paper. Trim orange paper ¼" from purple arch. Glue orange paper to box lid.
9. Use stick-on letters to spell "HAUNTED HOUSE OF PIZZA" on arch. Use black pen to write "A taste to die for …" on bottom of arch.
10. Use bat pattern to cut bat from remaining black paper. Use neon yellow pencil to draw eyes on bat. Glue bat to box lid.
11. Use craft glue to glue ribbon around side of box.

"BEARY" FUN TREATS

PUMPKIN BREAD

This ghostly guy is all set to help you deliver some delicious Halloween treats. The moist, spicy Pumpkin Bread is loaded with raisins and pecans for extra flavor. We baked ours in small cans for a nice size and shape. Perfect for carrying the mini loaves, tiny tote bags are cross stitched with cute little costumed bears.

3½ cups all-purpose flour
2 teaspoons baking soda
1½ teaspoons salt
1 teaspoon ground cinnamon
1 teaspoon ground nutmeg
¼ teaspoon ground allspice
¼ teaspoon ground ginger
¼ teaspoon ground cloves
2 cups granulated sugar
1 cup firmly packed brown sugar
1 cup vegetable oil
4 eggs
⅔ cup water
1 can (16 ounces) pumpkin
1 cup raisins
1 cup chopped pecans

Preheat oven to 350 degrees. In a medium bowl, stir together first 8 ingredients. In a large bowl, mix together sugars and oil. Add eggs and water; stir until well blended. Stir in pumpkin. Add dry ingredients to sugar mixture; stir until smooth. Stir in raisins and pecans. Spoon batter into 7 greased and floured 16-ounce cans, filling each can ⅔ full. Place cans on a baking sheet and bake 50 to 55 minutes or until a toothpick inserted in center of bread comes out clean. Transfer to a wire rack; cool in cans 10 minutes. Remove bread from cans; cool completely. Store in an airtight container.

Yield: 7 mini loaves bread

HALLOWEEN TOTES

Each design was stitched on a Rustico (14 ct) Janlynn® Personal-Wares® Lil' Tote. Two strands of floss were used for Cross Stitch and 1 for all other stitches.

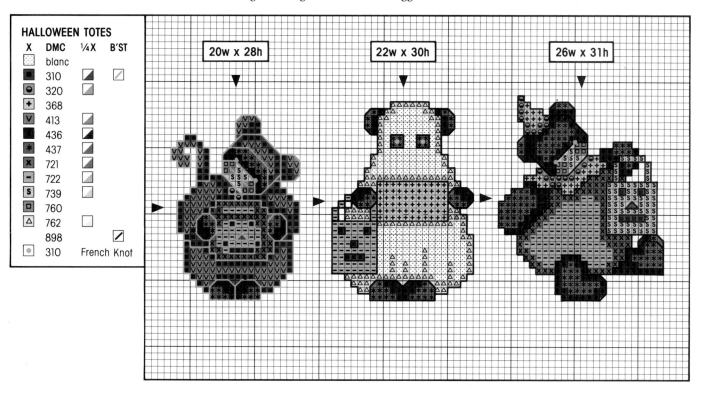

HALLOWEEN TOTES

X	DMC	¼X	B'ST
	blanc		
■	310		
⊙	320		
+	368		
V	413		
■	436		
✳	437		
X	721		
-	722		
S	739		
□	760		
△	762		
	898		
⊙	310	French Knot	

20w x 28h   22w x 30h   26w x 31h

GOBLIN SNACK WREATH

This spooky wreath features a basket filled with bags of sweet Cinnamon Snack Mix for guests or trick-or-treaters. Goblins of all sizes will gobble up this tasty snack!

CINNAMON SNACK MIX

- 2 cups toasted oat cereal
- 2 cups small pretzels
- 2 cups dry-roasted peanuts
- 1 cup raisins
- ½ cup granulated sugar
- ½ cup firmly packed brown sugar
- ½ cup sour cream
- ¾ teaspoon ground cinnamon
- 1 teaspoon vanilla extract

In a large bowl, combine cereal, pretzels, peanuts, and raisins.

In a medium saucepan, combine next 4 ingredients. Stirring constantly, cook over medium-low heat until sugar dissolves. Attach candy thermometer to pan, making sure thermometer does not touch bottom of pan. Increase heat to medium and bring to a boil. Cook, without stirring, until syrup reaches hard ball stage (approximately 250 to 268 degrees). Test about ½ teaspoon syrup in ice water. Syrup should form a hard ball in ice water and remain hard when removed from the water. Remove from heat and stir in vanilla. Pour syrup over cereal mixture, stirring until well coated. Spread on a buttered baking sheet. Cool completely. Break into pieces. Store in an airtight container.

Yield: about 9½ cups snack mix

HALLOWEEN WREATH

You will need a birch wreath, white Paper Capers™ twisted paper (untwisted), one 1″ dia. plastic foam ball for each ghost, purchased papier mâché pumpkin vine, basket with flat sides, white poster board, Design Master® glossy wood tone spray (available at craft stores or florist shops), small brown paper sacks, hole punch, white cotton string, black felt-tip marker, black colored pencil, florist wire, hot glue gun, and glue sticks.

1. For each ghost, cut a 10″ length of twisted paper. Place foam ball at center of paper. Fold long edges of paper over foam ball. Match short edges and fold paper in half over ball. To form head, tie a length of string into a bow around paper under ball. Draw eyes on head with black pencil. Trim bottom edges of paper into jagged edges.
2. For sign, cut a 2″w strip of poster board as long as front of basket; cut each end of strip into a jagged edge. Spray sign lightly with wood tone spray. For shading, spray a second coat along edges of sign; allow to dry. Write "for good little goblins" on sign with marker. Glue sign to front of basket.
3. Wire basket to wreath.
4. Arrange pumpkin vine and ghosts on wreath; use wire or glue to secure.
5. For each snack sack, fill sack half full with snack mix; fold top of sack 1½″ to back. Punch two holes 1″ apart ½″ from top of sack. Thread a length of string through holes and tie into a bow. Place snack sacks in basket.

FOR GOURMET GOBLINS

This Halloween, treat your grown-up friends to these delectable caramel apples. The traditional fall sweets become gourmet fare when dipped in white or semisweet chocolate and rolled in chopped pecans. The fancy fruit is packaged in sacks decorated to look like grinning jack-o'-lanterns.

GOURMET CARAMEL APPLES

12 craft sticks
 1 dozen medium Red Delicious apples
 3 bags (14 ounces each) caramels
 6 tablespoons water
28 ounces semisweet or white baking chocolate, coarsely chopped
 5 cups chopped pecans

Insert craft sticks into stem ends of apples. In a medium saucepan, combine caramels and water. Stirring constantly, cook over medium-low heat until smooth. Remove from heat. Holding each apple over saucepan, spoon caramel mixture over apples. Cool completely on greased waxed paper.

Stirring constantly, melt desired chocolate in a small saucepan over low heat. Remove from heat. Holding each caramel-coated apple over saucepan, spoon chocolate over apple. Roll in pecans. Return to waxed paper to cool completely. Store at room temperature in an airtight container.

Yield: 1 dozen caramel apples

JACK-O'-LANTERN SACKS

For each sack, you will need an orange gift sack, graphite transfer paper, black permanent marker, green curling ribbon, green tissue paper, tracing paper, and green construction paper.

1. Trace face and tag patterns, page 120, onto tracing paper. Cut out tag pattern.
2. Use transfer paper to transfer face pattern to sack. Color face with marker.
3. Stuff bottom of sack ¼ full with tissue paper. Place caramel apple wrapped in plastic wrap in sack; trim top of sack 2½″ below top of craft stick.

4. Tuck tissue paper in top of sack; gather top of sack around craft stick. Tie curling ribbon around top of sack.
5. For tag, use pattern to cut tag from construction paper. Write name on tag with marker. Make a hole in top of tag and thread tag onto curling ribbon. Curl ribbon ends.

GIVING THANKS

A lovely gift for a holiday hostess, these Sweet Potato Pies are a delicious way to end a traditional Thanksgiving dinner. The delightful dessert, with its flaky crust and buttery flavor, is a pleasing alternative to the usual pumpkin pie. As a thoughtful finishing touch, send along an apron adorned with colorful harvest motifs and a gentle reminder to give thanks for life's blessings.

SWEET POTATO PIES

CRUST

> 2 cups all-purpose flour
> 1 teaspoon salt
> ¾ cup vegetable shortening
> ½ cup cold water

FILLING

> 1½ pounds sweet potatoes, cooked, peeled, and mashed (about 3 cups)
> ¾ cup butter or margarine, softened
> 3 eggs
> 1 cup granulated sugar
> 1 can (5 ounces) evaporated milk
> ½ cup whole milk
> 1 tablespoon all-purpose flour
> 1 teaspoon vanilla extract
> ¼ teaspoon salt

For crust, stir together flour and salt in a medium bowl. Using a pastry blender or 2 knives, cut in shortening until mixture resembles coarse meal. Sprinkle with water; mix until a soft dough forms. Divide dough in half. On a lightly floured surface, use a floured rolling pin to roll out half of dough to ⅛-inch thickness. Transfer to a 9-inch pie plate and use a sharp knife to trim edge of dough. Repeat for remaining dough. Cover and set aside.

Preheat oven to 350 degrees. For filling, beat potatoes and butter in a large bowl. Stir in remaining ingredients. Pour filling into crusts. Bake 50 to 55 minutes or until a knife inserted off-center comes out clean. Cool completely on a wire rack. Store in an airtight container in refrigerator.

Yield: 2 pies, about 8 servings each

HARVEST APRON

You will need a light-colored apron, Pentel® Fabricfun™ Pastel Dye Sticks (available in sets at art supply stores), brown permanent felt-tip pen with fine point, graphite transfer paper, tracing paper, 1 yd of ⅜"w orange grosgrain ribbon, 1 yd of ⅛"w yellow satin ribbon, and washable fabric glue.

1. Wash, dry, and press apron.
2. Trace apron patterns, pages 120 and 121, onto tracing paper; use transfer paper to transfer patterns to apron.
3. Use brown pen to draw over transferred lines. Add pumpkin vines, wheat stems, and detail lines on wheat with pen.
4. Place apron on a protected surface. Following dye stick manufacturer's instructions, color design and letters the following colors:

> pumpkins - yellow shaded with orange
> pumpkin stems - lt green shaded with green
> wheat - gold shaded with brown
> rope - lt green shaded with green
> letters - yellow shaded with orange.

5. Heat-set design according to dye stick manufacturer's instructions.
6. Glue yellow ribbon to center of orange ribbon; allow to dry. Glue a length of ribbon along top edge of apron. Tie a length of ribbon into a bow and glue to top corner of apron.
7. To launder, follow glue and dye stick manufacturers' recommendations.

"Autumn Leaves" Candy

*S*wirls of orange and gold give pieces of Candy Corn Brittle the look of autumn leaves. A sweet combination of chewy candy corn and crunchy brittle, the treat makes a great hostess gift at Thanksgiving. For a bountiful offering, present it in a ribbon-tied box along with a handsome arrangement of fall flowers, grains, and foliage.

Candy Corn Brittle

- 1½ cups granulated sugar
- ½ cup light corn syrup
- ¼ cup water
- 2 tablespoons butter or margarine
- ½ teaspoon salt
- 1 teaspoon baking soda
- 1 cup candy corn

Butter sides of a 3-quart heavy saucepan or Dutch oven. Combine sugar, corn syrup, and water in pan. Stirring constantly, cook over medium-low heat until sugar dissolves. Using a pastry brush dipped in hot water, wash down any sugar crystals on sides of pan. Attach candy thermometer to pan, making sure thermometer does not touch bottom of pan. Increase heat to medium and bring to a boil. Do not stir while syrup is boiling. Continue to cook until syrup reaches hard crack stage (approximately 300 to 310 degrees) and turns light golden in color. Test about ½ teaspoon syrup in ice water. Syrup should form brittle threads in ice water and remain brittle when removed from the water. Remove from heat and add butter and salt; stir until butter melts. Add baking soda (syrup will foam); stir until soda dissolves. Stir candy corn into syrup. Pour syrup onto a large piece of buttered aluminum foil. Using 2 greased spoons, pull edges of warm candy until stretched thin. Cool completely. Break into pieces. Store in an airtight container.

Yield: about 1¼ pounds brittle

Autumn Arrangement

You will need a basket; a block of floral foam to fit in basket; sheet moss; desired artificial, dried, or preserved flowers, grains, and foliage (we used dried-look mums and mini daisies, silk maple leaves, preserved mini oak, dried wheat, and dried colonial peppergrass); 4 small ears of Indian corn; and raffia.

1. Place floral foam in basket. Cover foam with sheet moss.
2. Inserting stems into foam, arrange flowers, grains, and foliage in basket.
3. Tie ears of corn together with raffia; tie raffia into a bow. Arrange corn in front of basket.

CHEERY CHEESE STAR

*Y*ou'll spread lots
of Yuletide cheer with this
Christmas Cheese Star!
Molded in a traditional
holiday shape, the creamy
spread is lightly spiced with
red pepper and garlic and
garnished with cucumber
slices, sweet red pepper,
and fresh parsley. It's
perfect for taking along
to holiday parties.

CHRISTMAS CHEESE STAR

2½ cups (about 10 ounces)
    shredded sharp Cheddar cheese
1 carton (12 ounces) cottage cheese
1 package (8 ounces) cream cheese,
    softened
1 jar (4 ounces) diced pimientos,
    drained
2 tablespoons dried minced onion
½ teaspoon garlic powder
½ teaspoon ground red pepper
    Sweet red pepper, cucumber,
    and parsley for garnish

Line a 1-quart star-shaped mold with
plastic wrap. In a large bowl, combine
cheeses, pimientos, onion, garlic

powder, and red pepper using an
electric mixer. Spoon into prepared
mold. Cover and chill 1 hour. Invert
mold onto a serving plate. Remove
plastic wrap. Use a small star-shaped
aspic cutter to cut out stars from sweet
red pepper. Garnish cheese star with
cucumber slices, red pepper stars, and

parsley. Cover and refrigerate until
ready to present. Give with serving
instructions.

Yield: about 3¾ cups cheese spread

To serve: Let stand at room temperature
20 to 30 minutes or until softened.
Serve with crackers or bread.

Dipped in red- or green-tinted almond bark, Christmas Pretzels are a festive version of a popular snack. Our adorable Santa sack is just the thing for holding the pretzels — the "window" in his tummy provides a tantalizing peek at the treats inside! The colorful pretzels also make great edible ornaments for a tabletop tree.

CHRISTMAS PRETZELS

Vanilla-flavored almond bark
Green and red powdered food coloring or oil-based candy coloring
Assorted sizes of pretzels
White candy sprinkles

Stirring constantly, melt desired amount of almond bark in a small saucepan over low heat. Tint almond bark green. Using a fork, dip desired number of pretzels, one at a time, into almond bark, coating completely. Transfer to a wire rack with waxed paper underneath. Before almond bark hardens, decorate pretzels with candy sprinkles. Allow almond bark to harden. Repeat, tinting almond bark red.

SANTA SACK

You will need the following pieces of fabric: one 10″ x 18″ piece for sack, two 7″ x 9″ pieces for hat, two 5″ x 5½″ pieces for sleeves, four 4″ x 8½″ pieces for arms, and two 7″ squares for head.
You will also need one 9″ x 18″ piece of clear medium weight (8 gauge) vinyl (available at fabric stores), one 1″ x 10″ and two 1″ x 6½″ pieces of artificial lamb fleece, 1 yd of 1″w white cotton brush fringe, 18″ of 1″w satin ribbon for belt, 26″ of ½″w satin ribbon for drawstring, four 2½″ lengths of ¼″w metallic ribbon for belt buckle, paper-backed fusible web, tissue paper, thread to match fabrics, one 2½″ x 5¾″ piece of cardboard for bottom of sack, heavy thread (buttonhole twist), two ⅜″ dia. black shank buttons for eyes, one ⅝″ dia. red button for nose, one 1″ dia. white pom-pom, polyester fiberfill, tracing paper, fabric marking pencil, compass, seam ripper, hot glue gun, glue sticks, and fabric glue.

1. For sack, cut a 9″ x 18″ piece from web. Matching 1 long edge of web to 1 long edge (bottom) of 10″ x 18″ fabric piece, follow manufacturer's instructions to fuse web to wrong side of fabric.
2. For belt, use fabric glue to glue 1″w ribbon to right side of fused fabric with 1 long edge (bottom) of ribbon 3½″ from bottom edge of fabric.
3. For window pattern, cut a 2″ square from tracing paper. Center pattern over belt and draw around pattern; cut out square.
4. Place fabric, web side up, on ironing board. Place vinyl over webbed area. Being careful not to touch vinyl with iron, use a pressing cloth and a low iron setting to fuse vinyl to fabric.
5. Use fabric glue to glue metallic ribbon lengths along edges of window.
6. (*Note:* Use a ¼″ seam allowance unless otherwise indicated. To sew vinyl, use tissue paper on both sides of seam; tear away tissue paper after sewing.) Matching right sides and short edges, fold fabric in half. Sew short edges together to form a tube. Finger press seam open.
7. With seam at center back, finger press tube flat. Sew raw edges together at bottom (vinyl end) of tube.
8. Match each finger-pressed line at side of sack to seam at bottom of sack; sew across each corner 1½″ from point (Fig. 1). Trim each corner 1″ from point.

Fig. 1

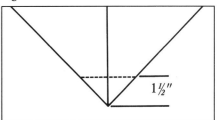

9. For casing, press top edge of sack ¼″ to wrong side; press ¾″ to wrong side again. Stitch ⅝″ from top edge. Turn sack right side out. Use seam ripper to open casing on outside of sack at seamline. Thread ½″w ribbon through casing. Place cardboard in bottom of sack.
10. For head pattern, use compass to draw a 5½″ dia. circle on tracing paper; cut out. Use pattern and follow Sewing Shapes, page 122, to make head from 7″ fabric squares. Stuff head with fiberfill; sew final closure by hand.

Continued on page 108

SANTA SACK (continued)

11. For nose, use heavy thread and come up through center of head. Thread needle through red button and go down through head approx. $\frac{1}{8}''$ away. Pull thread tightly to create a dimple in head. Repeat to make several stitches. Knot thread and trim ends. Repeat for eyes using black buttons.

12. For beard, cut four 8″ lengths from brush fringe. Hot glue one 8″ length of fringe along bottom edge of head. Repeat to layer remaining 8″ lengths, overlapping lengths approx. $\frac{1}{2}''$. For mustache, cut two $\frac{1}{2}''$ lengths from remaining fringe; hot glue under nose.

13. For hat, use pattern and follow Tracing Patterns and Sewing Shapes, page 122, to make hat from 7″ x 9″ pieces.

14. For trim on hat, use fabric glue to glue 1″ x 10″ fleece piece around bottom of hat. Hot glue pom-pom to point of hat. Hot glue hat to head.

15. Whipstitch back of head below hat to casing at center front of sack.

16. For each sleeve, match right sides and fold one 5″ x 5½″ piece in half lengthwise. Sew long edges together; turn right side out. Press 1 short edge (top) $\frac{1}{4}''$ to wrong side.

17. For trim on each sleeve, use fabric glue to glue one 1″ x 6½″ fleece piece around bottom of sleeve.

18. Use arm pattern and follow Tracing Patterns and Sewing Shapes, page 122, to make 2 arms from 4″ x 8½″ fabric pieces. Stuff arms with fiberfill to within 2″ of opening.

19. Insert 1 arm into 1 sleeve, matching top of arm with top of sleeve. Place sleeve on side of sack with top edge of sleeve 1″ below top of sack; whipstitch top of sleeve to sack, catching top of arm in stitching. Repeat for remaining sleeve and arm.

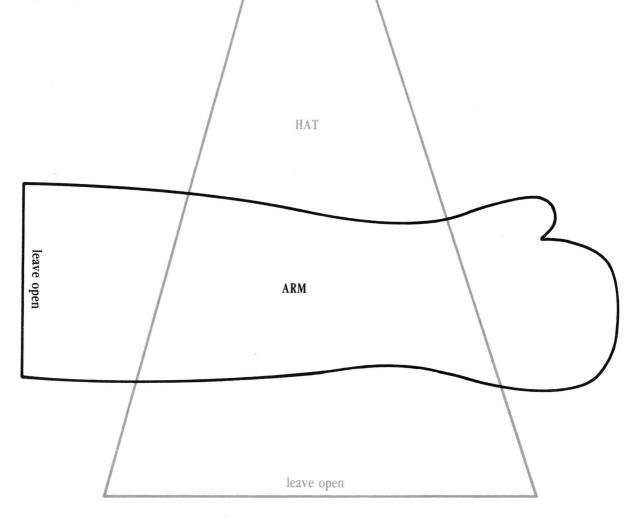

HAT

ARM

leave open

leave open

CHRISTMAS CORN BREAD

Great for sharing with neighbors at Christmastime, Zucchini Corn Bread has a mild flavor that's delicious with almost any meal. Zucchini and onion add garden-fresh goodness to the moist bread. For a presentation that's both practical and pretty, deliver the bread in the baking pan for easy reheating. A clear cellophane wrapper dressed up with festive ribbon and trims provides a glimpse of the good tastes to come.

ZUCCHINI CORN BREAD

    3 cups cornmeal
    ½ cup all-purpose flour
    2 teaspoons baking powder
    1 teaspoon salt
 1½ cups cottage cheese
 1½ cups milk
    1 cup butter or margarine, melted
    4 eggs
    1 cup finely chopped zucchini
    1 cup finely chopped onion

Preheat oven to 375 degrees. In a large bowl, stir together first 4 ingredients. In a medium bowl, whisk together next 4 ingredients. Add cottage cheese mixture and remaining ingredients to dry ingredients; stir just until moistened. Pour into 2 greased 8-inch square baking pans. Bake 25 to 30 minutes or until golden brown. Cool completely in pans. Cover and refrigerate until ready to present. Give with reheating instructions.

Yield: 2 pans corn bread

To reheat: Preheat oven to 350 degrees. Cover and bake 30 to 35 minutes or until heated through. Serve warm.

CLASSROOM PARTY TREE

*J*ust the thing for a classroom Christmas party, this little tree will delight children. The edible cookie ornaments are decorated with colorful candy-coated chocolate chips and attached to the tree with satin ribbon ties. A pretty bead garland completes the trimmings.

SUGAR COOKIE ORNAMENTS

  1 cup butter or margarine, softened
1½ cups granulated sugar
  1 egg
  1 teaspoon vanilla extract
2¾ cups all-purpose flour
  ¼ teaspoon salt
  1 package (10 ounces) candy-
      coated mini chocolate chips

Preheat oven to 350 degrees. In a large bowl, cream butter and sugar until fluffy. Add egg and vanilla; beat until smooth. In a medium bowl, stir together flour and salt. Add dry ingredients to creamed mixture; stir until a soft dough forms. Shape dough into 1-inch balls and place 3 inches apart on a greased baking sheet. Press each ball into a 2½-inch-diameter circle. Use a drinking straw to make a hole in top of each cookie. Press about 1 teaspoon chocolate chips onto each cookie. Bake 8 to 10 minutes or until edges are light golden brown. Transfer to a wire rack to cool completely. Store in an airtight container until ready to decorate tree.

Yield: about 5½ dozen cookies

FRUITY KUGEL

*P*ineapple and raisins lend fruity flavor to our delicious kugel made with egg noodles. A traditional Jewish dish, this dessert is similar to rice pudding in flavor. It's a nice way to help a friend celebrate Hanukkah, the Festival of Lights.

PINEAPPLE KUGEL

6 ounces medium egg noodles, cooked and drained (about 3 cups)

1 cup whipping cream

4 eggs, separated

½ cup granulated sugar

½ teaspoon salt

½ teaspoon ground cinnamon

¼ teaspoon ground nutmeg

⅔ cup raisins

1 can (15 ounces) crushed pineapple, drained

1 tablespoon vanilla extract

Preheat oven to 350 degrees. In a large bowl, stir together noodles, cream, egg yolks, sugar, salt, cinnamon, and nutmeg. Stir in raisins, pineapple, and vanilla. In a medium bowl, beat egg whites until stiff. Fold egg whites into noodle mixture. Pour into a greased 7 x 11-inch glass baking dish. Bake 35 to 40 minutes or until top is light brown. Cover and store in refrigerator until ready to present. Give with reheating instructions.

Yield: 12 to 15 servings

To reheat: Cover and bake in a preheated 350-degree oven 35 to 40 minutes or until heated through.

Holiday "Whine" Basket

APPLE-CINNAMON WINE

> 1 bottle (750 ml) dry white wine
> 3 medium Granny Smith apples, peeled, cored, and finely chopped (about 4½ cups)
> ½ cup granulated sugar
> ½ teaspoon ground cinnamon

In a 2-quart container, combine all ingredients; stir until sugar dissolves. Cover and refrigerate 1 month to allow flavors to blend. Use cheesecloth to strain wine, reserving ½ cup apples for Apple-Cinnamon Cheese Ball if desired (recipe follows). Serve wine chilled.

Yield: about 3 cups wine

APPLE-CINNAMON CHEESE BALL

> 1 package (8 ounces) cream cheese, softened
> ½ cup apples from Apple-Cinnamon Wine (recipe this page)
> ¼ cup chopped pecans
> ¼ teaspoon ground cinnamon
> Chopped pecans

In a medium bowl, combine cream cheese, apples, ¼ cup pecans, and cinnamon. Shape into a ball and roll in pecans. Wrap cheese ball in plastic wrap and refrigerate 8 hours or overnight to allow flavors to blend. Give with serving instructions.

Yield: 1 cheese ball

To serve: Let stand at room temperature 20 to 30 minutes or until softened. Serve with vanilla wafers or sugar cookies.

WAX-SEALED WINE BOTTLE

You will need paraffin, 20" of cotton string, double boiler (or electric frying pan and metal can), crayon with paper removed (to color wax), masking tape, and newspaper.

Caution: Do not melt paraffin over an open flame or directly on burner.

1. Cover work area with newspaper. Melt paraffin to a depth of 2½" in double boiler over hot water or in a can placed in an electric frying pan filled with water. Add pieces of crayon to melted paraffin until desired color is achieved.

2. (*Note:* Make sure cork is firmly inserted in bottle or cap is screwed on tightly.) On neck of bottle, center string on front; bring string around bottle to back and twist lengths tightly together (Fig. 1a). Keeping string taut, bring both ends over top of bottle (Fig. 1b); tape ends to front of bottle 4" below top.

Fig. 1a

back

Fig. 1b

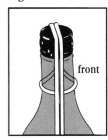

front

3. Dip approx. 2" of top of bottle in melted paraffin. Allowing paraffin to harden slightly between coats, continue dipping bottle until string is well coated. Remove tape; trim ends of string.

4. To break wax seal, pull string up toward top of bottle and unwrap string.

PATTERNS

"PARTY" ICE BUCKET
(Page 7)

"HUG ME" SWEATSHIRT
(Page 9)

114

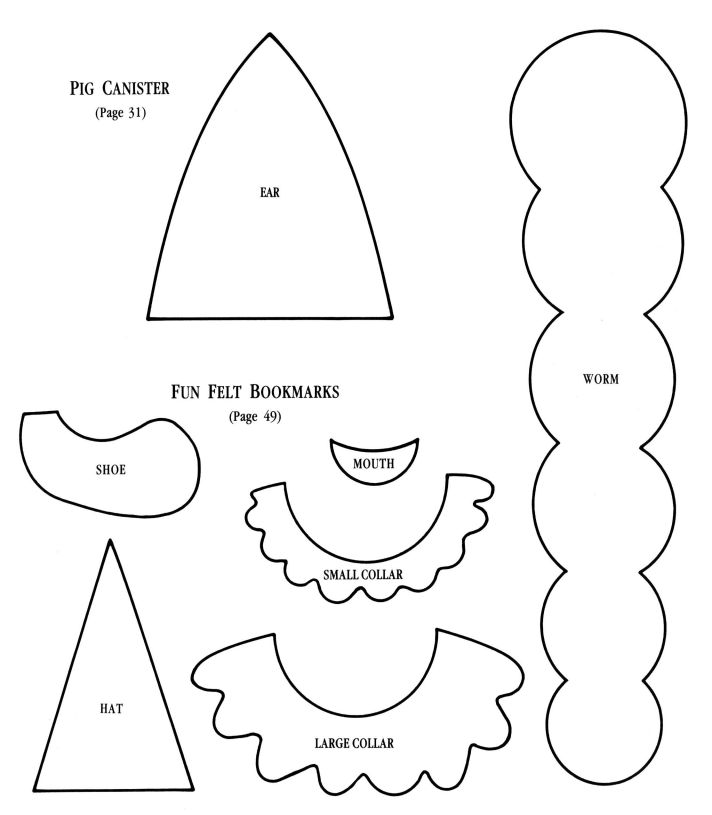

PIG CANISTER
(Page 31)

EAR

WORM

FUN FELT BOOKMARKS
(Page 49)

SHOE

MOUTH

SMALL COLLAR

HAT

LARGE COLLAR

PATTERNS (continued)

HUMPTY DUMPTY BREAD
(Page 53)

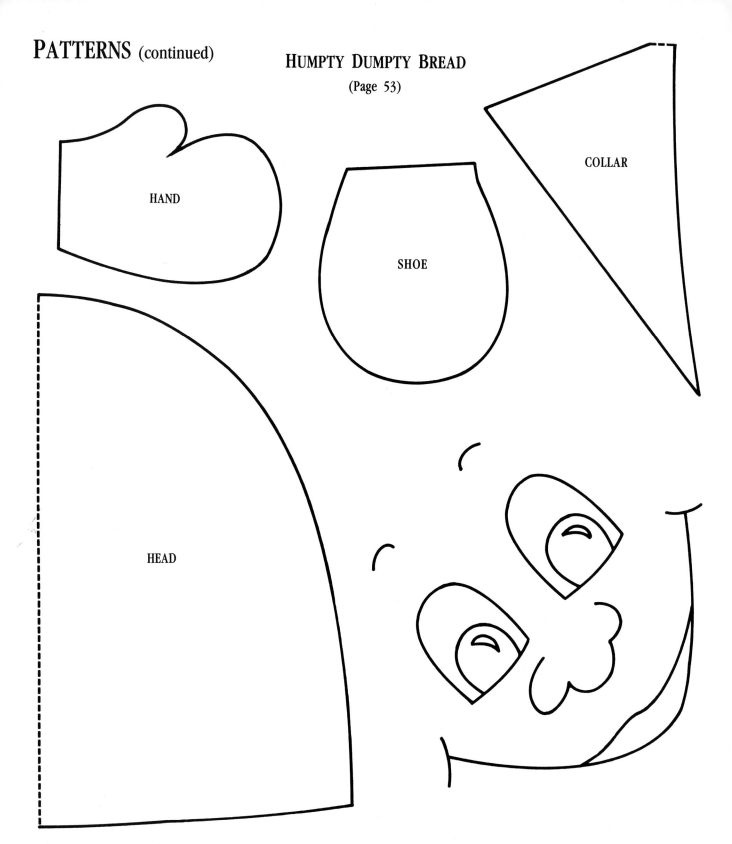

HAND

SHOE

COLLAR

HEAD

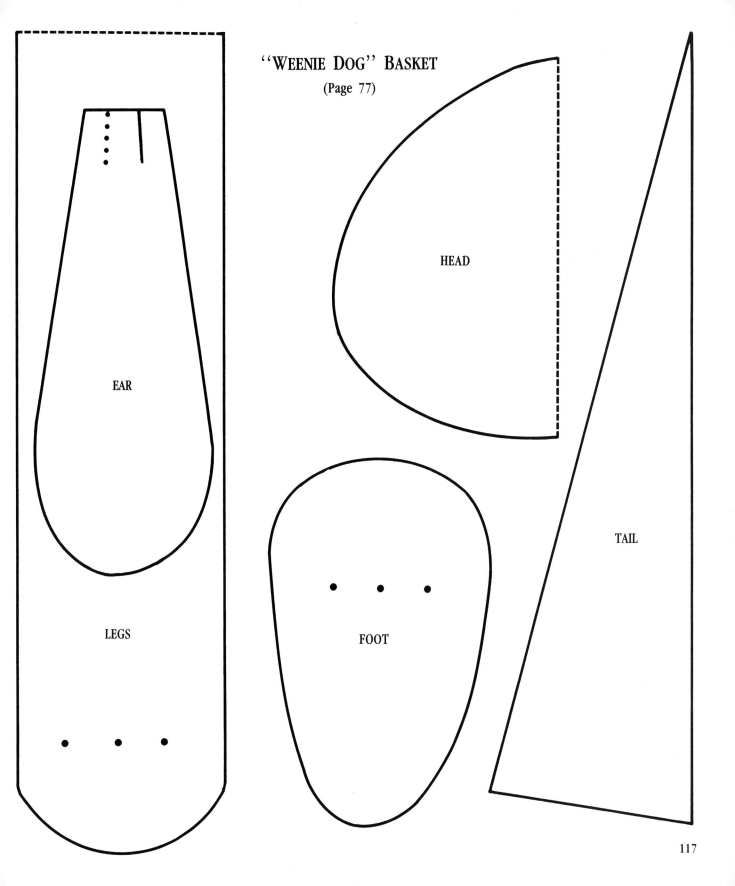

"WEENIE DOG" BASKET

(Page 77)

HEAD

EAR

TAIL

LEGS

FOOT

PATTERNS (continued)

UNCLE SAM CANISTER

(Page 79)

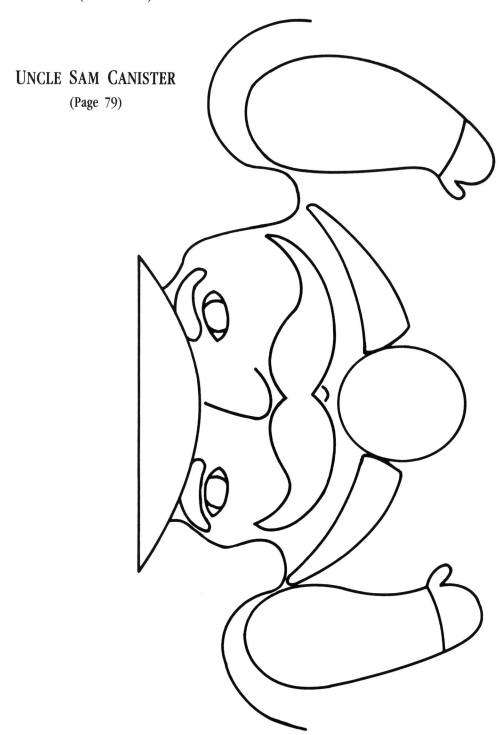

HALLOWEEN PIZZA BOX

(Page 97)

BAT

ARCH

WINDOW

GHOST

PATTERNS (continued)

JACK-O'-LANTERN SACKS
(Page 101)

FACE

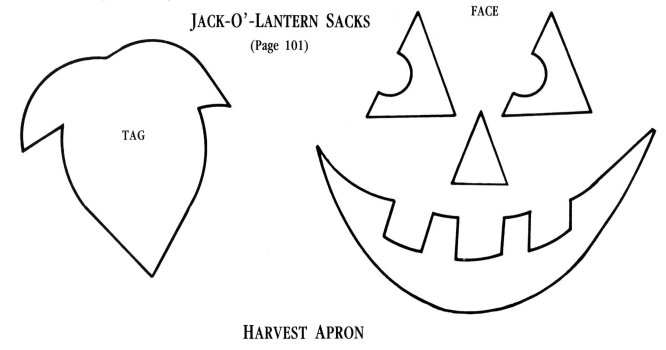

TAG

HARVEST APRON
(Page 103)

IN ALL THINGS....

GIVE THANKS

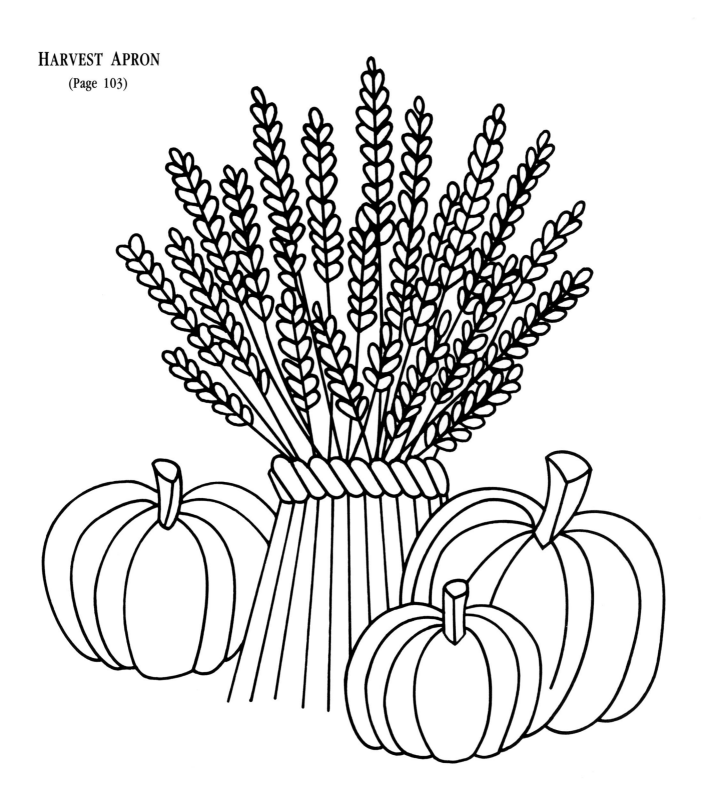

GENERAL INSTRUCTIONS

TRACING PATTERNS

When one-half of pattern (indicated by dashed line on pattern) is shown, fold tracing paper in half and place fold along dashed line of pattern. Trace pattern half, marking all placement symbols and markings; turn folded paper over and draw over all markings. Unfold pattern and lay flat. Cut out pattern.

When entire pattern is shown, place tracing paper over pattern and trace pattern, marking all placement symbols and markings. Cut out pattern.

SEWING SHAPES

1. Center pattern on wrong side of 1 fabric piece and use fabric marking pencil to draw around pattern. DO NOT CUT OUT SHAPE.
2. Place fabric pieces right sides together. Leaving an opening for turning, carefully sew pieces together directly on pencil line.
3. Leaving a $\frac{1}{4}''$ seam allowance, cut out shape. Clip seam allowance at curves and corners. Turn shape right side out. Use the rounded end of a small crochet hook to completely turn small areas.

FABRIC BAG

1. To determine width of fabric needed, add $\frac{1}{2}''$ to finished width of bag; to determine length of fabric needed, double the finished height of bag and add $1\frac{1}{2}''$. Cut fabric the determined width and length.
2. With right sides together and matching short edges, fold fabric in half; finger press folded edge (bottom of bag).

Using a $\frac{1}{4}''$ seam allowance and thread to match fabric, sew sides of bag together.
3. Press top edge of bag $\frac{1}{4}''$ to wrong side; press $\frac{1}{2}''$ to wrong side again and stitch in place.
4. For bag with a flat bottom, match each side seam to fold line at bottom of bag; sew across each corner 1″ from point (Fig. 1). Turn bag right side out.

Fig. 1

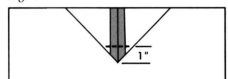

STENCILING

1. For stencil, trace pattern onto tracing paper. Use transfer paper to transfer design to center of tagboard. Place tagboard on cutting mat or a thick layer of newspapers. Use craft knife to cut out stencil.
2. (*Note:* Use removable tape to mask any cutout areas on stencil next to area being painted.) Hold or tape stencil in place. Use a clean, dry stencil brush for each color of paint. Dip brush in paint and remove excess paint on a paper towel. Brush should be almost dry to produce good results. Beginning at edge of cutout area, apply paint in a stamping motion. If desired, shade design by stamping additional paint around edge of cutout area. Carefully remove stencil and allow paint to dry.

GIFT BOX 1

Note: Use this technique to cover square or rectangular cardboard boxes that are already assembled, such as shoe boxes, department store gift boxes, or some candy boxes.

1. For box lid, refer to Fig. 1 to measure length and width of lid (including sides). Add $1\frac{1}{2}''$ to each measurement; cut wrapping paper the determined size.

Fig. 1

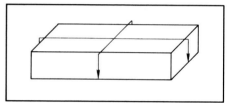

2. Place wrapping paper right side down on a flat surface; center box lid, top side down, on paper. For 1 short side of box lid, cut paper diagonally from corners to within $\frac{1}{16}''$ of lid (Fig. 2a). Fold short edge of paper up and over side of lid (Fig. 2b, page 123); crease paper along folds and tape edge in place inside lid. Repeat for remaining short side.

Fig. 2a

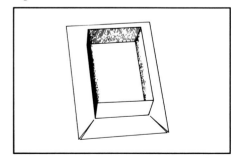

Fig. 2b

3. For 1 long side of box lid, fold paper as shown in Fig. 3; crease paper along folds. Fold paper up and over side of lid; crease paper along folds and tape edge in place inside lid. Repeat for remaining long side.

Fig. 3

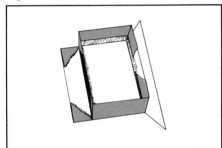

4. Repeat Steps 1 - 3 for bottom of box.

GIFT BOX 2

Note: Use this technique to cover cardboard boxes that are unassembled or are easily unfolded, such as cake boxes or mailing boxes.

1. Unfold box to be covered. Cut a piece of wrapping paper 1″ larger on all sides than unfolded box. Place wrapping paper right side down on a flat surface.

2. For a small box, apply spray adhesive to outside of entire box. Place box, adhesive side down, on paper; press firmly to secure.

3. For a large box, apply spray adhesive to bottom of box. Center box, adhesive side down, on paper; press firmly to secure. Applying spray adhesive to 1 section at a time, repeat to secure remaining sections of box to paper.

4. Use a craft knife to cut paper even with edges of box. If box has slits, use craft knife to cut through slits from inside of box.

5. Reassemble box.

CROSS STITCH

COUNTED CROSS STITCH (X)
Work 1 Cross Stitch to correspond to each colored square on the chart. For horizontal rows, work stitches in 2 journeys (Fig. 1a). For vertical rows, complete each stitch as shown in Fig. 1b. When the chart shows a Backstitch crossing a colored square (Fig. 1c), a Cross Stitch (Fig. 1a or 1b) should be worked first; then the Backstitch (Fig. 3) should be worked on top of the Cross Stitch.

Fig. 1a   Fig. 1b

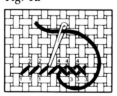

Fig. 1c

QUARTER STITCH (¼X)
Quarter Stitches are denoted by triangular shapes of color on the chart and on the color key. Come up at 1 (Fig. 2); then split fabric thread to go down at 2.

Fig. 2

BACKSTITCH (B'ST)
For outline detail, Backstitch (shown on chart and color key by black or colored straight lines) should be worked after the design has been completed (Fig. 3).

Fig. 3

FRENCH KNOT
Bring needle up at 1. Wrap floss once around needle and insert needle at 2, holding end of floss with non-stitching fingers (Fig. 4). Tighten knot; then pull needle through fabric, holding floss until it must be released. For a larger knot, use more strands; wrap only once.

Fig. 4

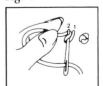

KITCHEN TIPS

MEASURING INGREDIENTS

Liquid measuring cups have a rim above the measuring line to keep liquid ingredients from spilling. Nested measuring cups are used to measure dry ingredients, butter, shortening, and peanut butter. Measuring spoons are used for measuring both dry and liquid ingredients.

To measure flour or granulated sugar: Spoon ingredient into nested measuring cup and level off with a knife. Do not pack down with spoon.

To measure confectioners sugar: Sift sugar, spoon lightly into nested measuring cup, and level off with a knife.

To measure brown sugar: Pack sugar into nested measuring cup and level off with a knife. Sugar should hold its shape when removed from cup.

To measure dry ingredients equaling less than ¼ cup: Dip measuring spoon into ingredient and level off with a knife.

To measure butter, shortening, or peanut butter: Pack ingredient firmly into nested measuring cup and level off with a knife.

To measure liquids: Use a liquid measuring cup placed on a flat surface. Pour ingredient into cup and check measuring line at eye level.

To measure honey or syrup: For more accurate measurement, lightly spray measuring cup or spoon with cooking spray before measuring so the liquid will release easily from cup or spoon.

TESTS FOR CANDY MAKING

To determine the correct temperature of cooked candy, use a candy thermometer and the cold water test. Before each use, check the accuracy of your candy thermometer by attaching it to the side of a small saucepan of water, making sure thermometer does not touch bottom of pan. Bring water to a boil. Thermometer should register 212 degrees when water begins to boil. If it does not, adjust the temperature range for each candy consistency accordingly.

When using a candy thermometer, insert thermometer into candy mixture, making sure thermometer does not touch bottom of pan. Read temperature at eye level. Cook candy to desired temperature range. Working quickly, drop about ½ teaspoon of candy mixture into a cup of ice water. Use a fresh cup of water for each test. Use the following descriptions to determine if candy has reached the correct consistency:

Soft Ball Stage (234 to 240 degrees): Candy can be rolled into a soft ball in ice water but will flatten when held in your hand.

Firm Ball Stage (242 to 248 degrees): Candy can be rolled into a firm ball in ice water but will flatten if pressed when removed from the water.

Hard Ball Stage (250 to 268 degrees): Candy can be rolled into a hard ball in ice water and will remain hard when removed from the water.

Soft Crack Stage (270 to 290 degrees): Candy will form hard threads in ice water but will soften when removed from the water.

Hard Crack Stage (300 to 310 degrees): Candy will form brittle threads in ice water and will remain brittle when removed from the water.

CANNING INSTRUCTIONS

Wash jars and bands in hot, soapy water; rinse well. Place jars on a rack in a Dutch oven or stockpot. Place bands in a saucepan; cover jars and bands with water. Bring water to a boil; boil 10 minutes. Prepare lids according to manufacturer's instructions. Remove pans from heat, leaving jars, lids, and bands in hot water until ready to use. Immediately before filling, remove jars from hot water and drain well. Fill hot jars to within ¼ inch of tops. Wipe jar rims and threads with a clean, dry cloth. Quickly cover with lids and screw bands on tightly. For jellies, invert jars 5 minutes; turn upright to cool. For jams, butters, marmalades, and conserves, use water-bath method as directed by USDA, referring to recipe for processing time. When jars have cooled, check seals. Lids should be curved down or remain so when pressed.

SOFTENING BUTTER OR MARGARINE

To soften butter, remove wrapper from butter and place on a microwave-safe plate. Microwave 1 stick 20 to 30 seconds at medium-low power (30%).

SOFTENING CREAM CHEESE

To soften cream cheese, remove wrapper from cream cheese and place on a microwave-safe plate. Microwave 1 to 1½ minutes at medium power (50%) for one 8-ounce package or 30 to 45 seconds for one 3-ounce package.

SUBSTITUTING HERBS

To substitute fresh herbs for dried, use 1 tablespoon fresh chopped herbs for ½ teaspoon dried herbs.

WHIPPING CREAM

For greatest volume, chill a glass bowl, beaters, and cream until well chilled before whipping. In warm weather, place chilled bowl over ice while whipping cream.

CUTTING COOKIE SHAPES

To cut out cookie shapes, dip cookie cutter in flour to keep dough from sticking to cutter.

ROLLING OUT PIE DOUGH

Tear off four 24-inch-long pieces of plastic wrap. Overlapping long edges, place two pieces of wrap on a slightly damp, flat surface; smooth out wrinkles. Place dough in center of wrap. Overlapping long edges of remaining pieces of wrap, cover dough. Use rolling pin to roll out dough 2 inches larger than diameter of pie plate. Remove top pieces of wrap. Invert dough into pie plate. Remove remaining pieces of wrap.

BEATING EGG WHITES

For greatest volume, beat egg whites at room temperature in a clean, dry metal or glass bowl.

SHREDDING CHEESE

To shred cheese easily, place wrapped cheese in freezer for 10 to 20 minutes before shredding.

EQUIVALENT MEASUREMENTS

1 tablespoon	=	3 teaspoons
⅛ cup (1 fluid ounce)	=	2 tablespoons
¼ cup (2 fluid ounces)	=	4 tablespoons
⅓ cup	=	5⅓ tablespoons
½ cup (4 fluid ounces)	=	8 tablespoons
¾ cup (6 fluid ounces)	=	12 tablespoons
1 cup (8 fluid ounces)	=	16 tablespoons or ½ pint
2 cups (16 fluid ounces)	=	1 pint
1 quart (32 fluid ounces)	=	2 pints
½ gallon (64 fluid ounces)	=	2 quarts
1 gallon (128 fluid ounces)	=	4 quarts

HELPFUL FOOD EQUIVALENTS

½ cup butter	=	1 stick butter
1 square baking chocolate	=	1 ounce chocolate
1 cup chocolate chips	=	6 ounces chocolate chips
2¼ cups packed brown sugar	=	1 pound brown sugar
3½ cups unsifted confectioners sugar	=	1 pound confectioners sugar
2 cups granulated sugar	=	1 pound granulated sugar
4 cups all-purpose flour	=	1 pound all-purpose flour
1 cup shredded cheese	=	4 ounces cheese
3 cups sliced carrots	=	1 pound carrots
½ cup chopped celery	=	1 rib celery
½ cup chopped onion	=	1 medium onion
1 cup chopped green pepper	=	1 large green pepper

RECIPE INDEX

CREDITS

To Magna IV Engravers of Little Rock, Arkansas, we say thank you for the superb color reproduction and excellent pre-press preparation.

We want to especially thank photographers Ken West and Mark Mathews of Peerless Photography, Little Rock, Arkansas, and Jerry R. Davis of Jerry Davis Photography, Little Rock, Arkansas, for their time, patience, and excellent work.

To the talented people who helped in the creation of the following recipes and projects in this book, we extend a special word of thanks.

Death by Chocolate Cake, page 39: Francine Kearns
Braided Cornmeal Bread, page 94: Glenda Warren
Pumpkin Bread, page 99: Leslye Boyce
''Ground Hog'' label, page 17: Kathleen Murphy

Grandparents' Mugs, page 87: Jorja Hernandez of
  Kooler Design Studio
Halloween Totes, page 99: Lorraine Birmingham

We extend a sincere thank you to the people who assisted in making and testing the projects in this book: Deborah Bashaw, Elaine Garrett, Cara Lea Gregory, Ginny Hogue, Pat Johnson, and Kathy Womack Jones.